Overcoming Common Problems

How
Confid

Carole Baldock

sheldon PRESS

For Nathan, Cassia and Alysse, with love: all things are possible

CAROLE BALDOCK is the mother of three children. She graduated from Liverpool John Moores University in 1993 and is now a full-time freelance writer. Author of *How to Succeed as a Single Parent*, as well as *Writing Reviews* and *Making Money from Writing* (How To Books), Carole has also written several schools information packs. At present she is editor of *Competitions Bulletin;* associate editor of *Orbis*; markets and competitions editor for the *Women Writers Network* and coordinator for Liverpool's Dead Good Poets Society.

First published in Great Britain in 2000 by
Sheldon Press
Holy Trinity Church
Marylebone Road
London NW1 4DU

British Library Cataloguing-in-Publication Data

A catalogue record for this book is available from the British Library

ISBN 0–85969–828–9

Typeset by Deltatype Limited, Birkenhead, Merseyside
Printed in Great Britain by
Biddles Ltd, Guildford and King's Lynn

Contents

Part 1 Parenting through the ages: childhood and growing up

Introduction: self-esteem, insecurity and confidence

Nobody is 100 per cent confident 100 per cent of the time in 100 per cent of situations – not even those who are so self-assured their initials should be G.O.D. Few people are afflicted with chronically low self-esteem, but most of us would appreciate another big helping of confidence, thank you very much. If we could collar the Good Fairy when our children are born, that's what would be top of the list, along with good looks, good luck, and a good chance of winning the lottery.

In confidence: it's important

Parents want their children to be happy, making the most of their lives; self-confidence is the answer to our prayers. What can we do to make sure they have it? Especially since we usually want them to have a better start in life than we ever did. Especially when we often feel insecure. Well, teaching is a good way to learn something, and by encouraging their children's confidence, parents can improve their own self-esteem.

Rough equation: feelings of insecurity = low self-esteem = lack of confidence. Everybody is born with self-esteem, but it needs nurturing. Sparing the rod doesn't spoil children, but sparing words does: lack of praise or approval. Then add constant, harsh criticism. Bruises heal eventually, but psychological wounds are likely to scar the mind. Communication is vital, yet there's often a huge gap between intention and perception. We see ourselves instilling values, whereas children feel our views are forced upon them. It can be rectified: more encouragement whenever the opportunity arises, rather than criticism, or indifference, which is even more chilling.

The problems of low self-esteem

Insecurity affects our idea of ourselves. Or rather, how we believe that others see us. People lacking self-esteem, whether classed as villains or victims, are felt to cause many of society's ills. 'Sugar and spice, and all things nice . . .' that's what little girls are made of. Or are they as horrible as little boys? Some parents seem to think that all children deliberately behave badly, purely to upset them. We've all witnessed horrific little scenes, from packed supermarkets to picnics in beauty spots, when furious parent and child lock horns. It can seem almost

1

dreadfully comic, some small mite giving as good as it gets: swearing, slapping and all. But violent anger is frequently unleashed in parents by the slightest misdeeds, exacerbated by the child's sobbing or frantic apologies. There are many reasons given for such behaviour: poverty; unemployment; broken homes; social exclusion. The result is inevitable: such children grow up to treat their children exactly the same. So do their children. All because of low self-esteem. What of the 'nature/nurture' argument? No matter what the environment, insecure children feel worthless, growing up to believe they are unloved, and unlovable. If you don't love yourself, why should anybody else? And no point in loving anybody else. A gloomy prospect, not just for the immediate family – each individual is part of society, which ranges from extreme violence at one end, to people claiming compensation and/or counselling for the slightest scratch, at the other.

Self-esteem and self-confidence can be differentiated: 'to have a good opinion of oneself' and 'reliance on one's own powers' respectively, according to *Chambers* Dictionary. A symbiotic relationship: knowing you can believe in yourself and your abilities makes you think well of yourself, and vice versa. However, people may think you have boundless self-confidence, whilst deep inside, you're one horrible, scary mess. It's the basis for umpteen famous books and films; the media is full of stories about successful people who are notoriously difficult to get on with and end up doing the dumbest things. We can be totally successful in one area: work, home or leisure, but continue to make a complete mess of the rest. Familiarity may breed contempt, but should make us contented with our accomplishments. Something has to give, i.e. change, and if you want things, or other people, to change, then you start by changing yourself. To cite one of the most ancient (and best) jokes of its kind: how many psychiatrists does it take to change a lightbulb? Only one – but the lightbulb really has to want to change.

The advantages of good self-esteem

Why are there some people for whom life is a bowl of cherries, with cream always on tap? How is it some people are so flaming lucky everything comes their way and nothing ever goes wrong for them? Try asking around; some people appreciate your comments, amused it appears so easy, pointing out their mistakes and failures. Or they'll be peeved, and describe, at length, all their hard work and sacrifices.

Characteristics of high and low self-esteem

Think of people you admire, and those whom you, frankly, cannot stand. What triggers those emotions? Qualities seen as bad you wouldn't admit to; the good you would like to possess, and want your children to have, e.g. resilience, dependability, being sociable, etc. Characteristics of people with low self-esteem often seem contradictory, helping them to avoid responsibility, such as the over-ambitious or the under-achiever.

Most people display these traits, on occasion, but mix in some confidence and it doesn't interfere too much with the quality of their way of life. Popular people are seen as strong and cheerful (a winning combination), and many seem to go through life sipping the best things from a silver spoon: first-class job, beautiful home, wonderful relationship with wife and family.

However, according to a recent survey, confident people are often rude; it's the insecure who are usually polite, indeed, over-apologetic. Although the former are occasionally blunt, impatient and unsympathetic towards those less fortunate, they're also aware that the latter (often in the majority) are envious. Hence 'tall poppy syndrome': they need cutting down to size, the boss who is so cocky the whole damn time, that pushy woman who's just been promoted.

Everyone feels there's too much work and not enough hours, wondering why they tolerate tricky relationships at home and/or at work. When you're confident, you don't put up with situations like that for long. Assertion means you'll change things; resilience means to accept nothing's going to change, and move on. Some people can never be satisfied, while others, with few material blessings, appear content. Seeking the answer to making the most of life is the thing to do in a brand new century, and with so many options in self-development, improving your confidence is within everybody's grasp. It's vital for parents because children model themselves on us; when your self-esteem is low, naturally, it affects them. But they'll manage, just as you always have . . . don't we want our children to have much better lives than ours?

Problem areas

Parenting today subjects us to a babel of voices, frequently contradictory, telling us what to do: the experts, our own parents, family, friends. Words of wisdom from the pros don't strike us as friendly when running counter to everybody else's. Then, before you know it, there's your own children. How we yearn for those first tottering steps, those initial sounds (which may or may not be something like 'Dada' or 'Mama'). How soon we wish they'd stay put in one place for a moment, or be quiet for a second. But what about our own experience, knowledge, observation, and instincts? Overwhelmed with advice and information, it's more useful to work out what's best for us, and our children, even when different from what everybody else does. If it doesn't work, try another way; remember the old saying: keep on doing what you do, keep on getting what you get, good or bad.

Searching for solutions

A quick glance at the contents page suggests bad news: three sections devoted to problems and only one for solutions? The overall aim is to suggest ways of helping children to be confident, maintain confidence or improve it. Poor self-esteem usually can be made better.

Doing the research was an eye-opener, including ego trips by authors so perfect, they knew that they knew all the answers. Plus meanderings through New Age theories: exactly what to say to children in words which would have you both in fits of laughter or frowning with disgust. Plus an overwhelmingly positive attitude: stiff upper lip immobilized by permanently putting on a happy face.

Yes, it looks like a minefield out there and one that needs to be explored, slowly and surely. Besides, according to one encouraging theory, when something starts moving into a different state, for example water changing into ice, it will affect the rest. It takes less than one-fifth to do it; nearly everybody, no matter how low their self-esteem, can manage to summon up that amount of confidence. An effort worth making, because confidence leads to success, and success ensures confidence, for you and your children.

Infant terrors: babies can affect self-confidence

When congratulating new parents on their first-born, there are two distinct reactions: huge beams, or a mumbled reply from somebody who looks like they've been modelling for Munch's painting 'The Scream' for the past 48 hours non-stop.

Babies come in all shapes and sizes, and temperaments

Temperament does not necessarily run in the family. The first child may sleep through the night from the words 'go to sleep, now', lap up all the food that's good for him, possess an equable temperament, and, if he cries, get over it in 43 seconds flat. That's no guarantee the second one will, or the third, if you haven't been put off. Some babies don't impinge much on your way of life, allegedly, but others barely sleep, requiring loads of attention and stimulation.

Scrutinize your baby's head. See any sign of a mark like '666'? Babies are NOT born evil, despite cases in the daily papers where criminals are thus described, before being sentenced to about one afternoon in jail. Babies feel discomfort and pain, fear, hunger and weariness. You may curse the day you were lumbered with this creature, but one thing's for certain (and a straw you cling to): they don't behave out of selfishness or spite or for revenge. It's never because they hate you. But when you're absolutely exhausted, nerves so frazzled you hear them fizzing away, it's horrifying to realize how much you loathe this red-faced, screeching bundle which will not sleep, will not eat and will NOT shut up.

Why is she acting like this? Why does she persist in making you feel so wretched the whole time? It feels like a vendetta. Easy to picture a kind of good versus evil situation, but that frame of mind makes matters worse. Some babies are awkward little blighters, but grow out of it eventually or become easier to get along with. Once you stop believing it's a clash of personalities, with help, advice and support and advice from family and friends, you'll get through. 'Good' babies aren't just for those few lucky parents, or for those with plenty of confidence.

A new life

As well try explaining Earth to a Martian as succeed in making somebody with no children understand what it's like to be a parent; it's a major life-changing event. Some women believe the 'f-word' stands for 'feminism', but the most ardent wimmin may revel (secretly) in the knowledge that the miracle of giving birth gives us the advantage over men, apart from the actual process, the ultimate in no pain, no gain. However, unlike previous generations, having led financially and socially independent lives, women now are less prepared for having children, the loss of freedom and greater responsibility. And there's something of a chasm between the childless and people with children. Having children frequently results in draining your confidence.

What turns this miracle so rapidly into your worst nightmare?

Wendy was a whiz-kid who coped with any problem, at work or play. Now, she looks like a zombie, conjured up by specials effects for the latest horror film. Designer wear a crumpled heap in an over-flowing clothes-basket, she meanders round in a dressing gown never designed to be worn morning, noon and night, and a pair of bedraggled, yellow, fluffy clogs.

Many home alone mothers suffer from health problems: depression, panic attacks even a breakdown. Working mothers have additional worries, like child care, plus the latest media survey: not staying home with baby affects the child's reading ability.

Looking on the bright side

A negative picture? Naturally, there are also good times. To raise confident children, they need to be given a good start, and think how this will benefit them, for example, years later, when they attend interviews. One popular strategy is to imagine future employers clad in their underwear, but what if they're pictured as nasty little brats? The faces and the deeds of the great and good are so familiar to us, but we'd never dream of thinking about them like that, though it's what we all have in common.

Few of us remember that far back, but parents do, usually glossing over the bad bits. Good memories last, because babies are incredible little creatures. One smile or giggle can enslave a complete stranger, making parents forget that the past 24 hours was wall-to-wall anguish. Within a few months to a year, most parents find their confidence is restored, maybe bigger and better than before, all the more easily passed on to their children.

Self-esteem in babies

All a brand new baby wants is nourishment and affection to feel secure, but it can soon be affected. When they do start yelling, let them exercise their lungs (although their capacity for wailing seems phenomenal); to pre-empt their needs is frustrating, and may cause problems in adulthood. Ignoring a distressed baby, leaving him to cry for ages may lead to him becoming quiet and passive, and result in depression as an adult. The more you yell, the more he's going to yell; where's he learning it from, after all?

Possibly more embarrassing is the way many infants adopt a comforter, often dummies but also a toy or a bit of blanket (keep a spare to avoid distress the minute it isn't to hand; material can be cut into a couple of pieces). Parents may struggle to dispose of it, but children eventually grow out of this stage. Then the trials of being on holiday and having to include a seat everywhere in pubs, etc. for Action Bunny make an entertaining anecdote, and it's the child's turn to be mortified.

Around seven months, he (the baby, not the bunny) starts to suffer from separation anxiety, which generally lasts until he's two, though many toddlers are clingy between 18 and 30 months. Some parents recall howls following them out of the room from birth onwards, though once they're out of sight, infants usually settle down. Boys are said to feel more internally than girls from birth and miss their mothers more, but, less able to express their emotions, they respond less easily. In turn, this affects the way adults react to boys, so they assume girls are more approved of.

Traditionally, father entertains baby, but is usually less demonstrative and/or talkative; mother provides more discipline However, as boys grow up, they need to see their dad in action, being kind and calm, as well as capable around the house. Under six years of age, a baby needs his mother or primary carer most; from 6 to 14, a father figure to look up to, and from 15 onwards, role models.

In theory, you can ensure babies have plenty of confidence: give them lots of love and affection; try massage as well as cuddles, and carry them around with you. Don't tell them off, because they aren't deliberately doing anything which calls for criticism. Instead, talk to them constantly, with love and admiration.

Make a habit of explaining things to them, OK, in words of one syllable. Get used to it, because you won't be able to escape the toddlers' incessant questioning. Once they've learnt the alphabet, don't they love that one letter: Y, Y, Y? And talk sense, which they understand as clearly as baby-talk. Do you want another grown up to overhear you being patronizing or utterly ridiculous? And it makes children feel embarrassed or inferior.

Boosting your own confidence

There's a lot to deal with, from getting used to your baby to sheer exhaustion; no wonder you end up feeling insecure, without having the further worry that everything you do will affect his self-esteem. Don't panic. The more uncertain you feel, the more stressed you get, and the more this affects the baby. Finding out about the stages of learning gives you a better idea of what to expect. Every baby is different.

Except when it comes to problems; they aren't unique to your child. Ask around; you'll be amazed how many new parents are sharing this leaky boat. And how many practised parents land safely. Asking for help is the most sensible thing to do, and shows you're being mature, not weak. Take heed of your own intuition too, and aim to be consistent, setting ground rules from the start for raising your children, and their self-confidence. Prior to the birth, what delightful reveries parents succumb to, what wonderful plans for the future. Since you ain't see nothin' yet, remember, these are your daydreams. Children have their own. Now and then, you won't like some of the things they do (or say). Fair enough; there's things you do which they really hate. A parent's love for their child is unconditional: good or bad, right or wrong, no matter what, you'll always love them. All you can do is make sure they always know that.

Toddling along . . .

Now the fun begins: wilful one-year-olds, terrible twos and traumatizing threes. Six to 18 months is the Age of the Explorer; once babies become mobile, you should see them go. Make the whole house a child-proof zone, EVERYTHING out of reach or locked away, including the cat. Minimalism never goes out of fashion, and what looks like a bare room to you is still full of exciting opportunities for a young child.

Most young children appear to be bursting with confidence. At this stage, because they're egocentric, the world does revolve round them. They seem to love putting on a show, revelling in attention, and it's often a charming sight: small, self-possessed person chatting up everybody on the train, under the indulgent eye of mama and papa. Or when a shy child is coaxed into being a little more forthcoming. But it doesn't take much for them to get carried away, delightful imp transformed into little demon; nobody likes Bossy Boots or Crybaby. They might also have been behaving badly all along, blithely tormenting other children and upsetting little old ladies, despite constant pleading, nagging or threats.

Yes, life now takes a tricky turn, and discipline needs to be introduced as children begin to learn about right and wrong. Whatever heinous crime they commit, assure them of your love, although it's easy to forget when they make a holy show of you. Victoria Wood describes this nightmare as taking a two-year-old to visit somebody who hates children and collects porcelain. Why ask for trouble? Arrange to meet in the park, or other neutral territory.

Temper, temper

In families where people are volatile, things blow up, blow over, then everything's restored to normal. Outbursts are almost refreshing, providing we're careful about the things we say. In other households, there's constant rows, even violence, or perennial sulking and a bad atmosphere. Some of us repress anger, whilst others lose their temper over the least little thing, crying and screaming, yelling and stamping (what do they do when catastrophe strikes?). Sometimes, counting to 100 in Mandarin Chinese wouldn't give you time to calm down, but being completely out of control is frightening, especially for toddlers. They're fascinated when they see other children in a temper, sympathetic when they're in tears, and can be helped to recognize emotion in others and understand their own through bedtime stories incorporating such situations. Encourage them to use their imagination, underlining the difference between reality and make-believe without equating telling stories with telling lies.

Imagine how frustrating life must be for young children so much of the time. They feel passionately about everything, but are constantly thwarted, being unable to do what they want, say what it is they want. Tantrums seem inevitable. Parents are only human, and tend to react by either throwing a wobbler themselves, or whining on in an absolutely desperate attempt to appeal to the child's better nature. The usual suggestions are to 'ignore it' or 'distract them'. With children being individuals, different strategies apply (see pp. 44–7).

It ain't what you do, it's the way that you do it

Make the most of your children's company by encouraging them to give you a hand with the chores. The novelty soon wears off, but they get into the habit, and it gives you a chance to chat about all kinds of things. It's the ideal age; they're starting to think things out, to learn from what you're doing and what you're saying. Show them what to do, then let them get on with it, ready to help out if asked. Praise them for their efforts, even if the results aren't up to your usual immaculate standards. Resist the compulsion to do it all again immediately the right way, and right in front of them, undermining their confidence. To you, if a job's worth doing, it's worth doing well, but at their age, this is a practice session; no need to make children feel useless.

It's easy to regard things like clumsiness as mortal sins when you're tired or in a hurry. But make it clear that it's NOT the child who's wrong or bad or stupid, even if that's what you feel about what they've done. Explain, briefly, that you're cross about what's happened – not oodles of babble with psychological undertones; if this is in public, think what it must sound like to other people. When you feel punishment is justified, carry it out there and then, so that the child can associate it with what was wrong.

> Kevin's in big trouble with his mum, who's trying to get him used to playschool because she's looking for a job. She's just made friends with Sharon's mother, who's opened up a new boutique, but Kevin swiped Sharon's sweets and made her cry. Instead of making him hand his over, the following week, he's expected to present her with a big gift-wrapped box of Belgian truffles. They end up squashed in the ensuing (and very noisy) tug of war.

Aiming for the right consistency

Discipline provides a framework and security for toddlers, and parents are urged to be consistent, but what strikes you as crime of the century when you're worn out and fed up, may seem quite amusing another time. But once you warn a child not to do something and they go right ahead, don't carry on making excuses, carry out what you said you would do. Two warnings, tops. They know they've done wrong, they've had a chance to consider the consequences. Don't chicken out.

Yes, we all do it, in the vain hope that children will give up and then you won't have to go to the bother of playing the stern parent, risking a huge argument which upsets everybody. Give toddlers an inch and they take a mile. When they're grown up, bad habits ingrained, they are much more eloquent: 'Honest, I'll pay you back as soon as I can. Yes, it really, really is the very last time I'll need to borrow money off you.'

It's not as if you have to warn children that if they don't give over, they'll be transported to Australia. Sending them to their room for a while gives both of you a breathing space, and you can't call it imprisonment; children are usually content to be there, when not in a temper. However, five minutes is an eternity for them, and for you. It's been suggested that you make it one minute for each year of their age, e.g. seven minutes for a seven-year-old, and wait quietly outside the door. Not that you'll have much chance to calm down if you can hear them trashing the room, or everything goes ominously quiet. As for smacking, most parents have had the odd slap as a child, and doled them out, usually when a child suddenly does something dangerous, like run into the road. When he has narrowly avoided being mown down, caused mass panic, and been retrieved with wild relief, a smack is more of a surprise than a lesson. With so many problems at this age, it's hard to hang on to your temper, and avoid lashing out. Do as you would be done by. The more you smack a child, the more he takes it as the norm, and starts hitting other children because that's what you do when you're annoyed, or upset or scared. And that's what your grandchildren will get.

Model parents

In theory, we know all about setting a good example, but can't always manage it. Not all the time. With a new baby, we proudly point out those features which resemble ours, and as they grow up, which of our characteristics they've inherited: 'Bright? You're telling me. Gets it from our side of the family, naturally.' Children instinctively model themselves on parents, adopting (and adapting) their behaviour: edgy parent = nervous daughter; reliable parent = dependable son. It's a huge shock overhearing your children at play, because their gift for mimicry is astonishing. Talk about seeing ourselves as others see us: they use our exact phrases and tone of voice, and it sounds horrible: nagging, bad-tempered, moaning or whining.

Patience is a virtue, and a blessing if you can hang on to it. There are so many war zones, with getting toddlers to eat properly and potty training them. And trying to make them go to sleep, then get them ready to go out, or stop fighting with their siblings and poking the cat. How much easier life will be once they start playschool.

Venturing out: from playschool to starting school

Wasn't it a man (Sartre?) who proclaimed that 'hell is other people'? Most women would amend that to 'hell is other people's children'. Parenting is never black and white, even in books, but being afflicted with the 'arrogance of rightness' doesn't help children, especially outside the home.

Hello, cruel world: the need for social skills

By the time they're two or three (18 months, if toilet trained) you can pack children off to playgroups, or playschools, which often aim to be primary school in miniature. They're expected to have acquired certain skills, in particular, socializing with other children, but they come into contact with attitudes different from those to which they're accustomed, encountering toddlers who are generally hostile or clingy. Confident children shrug this off, sticking to the company of those they like. The insecure find other children hard going: their behaviour affects them; the touchy ones become touchier. Some parents immediately think: 'You must admit, they're just asking for trouble', though never of their own child. It's not in the least correct to refer to a 'victim mentality', but even young children are seen as 'asking for it' (see pp. 101–4 on body language), which they unconsciously reveal in their posture, attitude and behaviour. They grow up believing they must deserve being stuck inside a vicious circle, habitually thinking they sport a sign saying 'Please don't kick me'. Others read it as: 'kick me – hard'.

Improve matters by equipping the less confident with skills to deal with the treatment doled out by other children. And as for their parents, there are those well meant comments wrapped around criticism:

> Leo insists on inviting the whole class home on his birthday. His mum feels it would be unkind to refuse, although some of the children, well . . . 'Chris, dear, I know you're shy, but you really must make some effort to join in, you know. You don't want to spoil the party now, do you?'

While the children's world comprises family and friends, it's not always much of a problem. The widening social circle makes them more vulnerable, having to deal with people who are far less understanding, and far more critical. Other children don't make allowances because they don't know how, or rather, don't understand.

Pushy parents

When you accompany your offspring to toddler group, the other children are often those yours have grown up with, as it were, from baby clinics, etc., when you've struck up friendships with their mothers. Or not; it isn't only parents who stay together for the sake of the children. Whilst the kids are all right, i.e. the best of friends, that's no guarantee two sets of parents will get on, especially when each has different ideas of the best ways of bringing up baby. This really brings out the competitive streak in parents; how many celebrities claim they felt they could never do anything right?

Encourage children to work as hard as they can, to strive to do their best, but help them along with large dollops of praise, reining in the criticism. Failure of any kind is punishment enough, without any further comment from you. Many mistakes are minor slip-ups, not major tragedies, and shouldn't be regarded in the same light, though there's always a lesson to be learned: to do something wrong or bad does not mean you are wholly a bad person.

Playing up

Until the age of three, children play *in* the company of others, rather than playing *with* them. Any interaction is usually squabbling, which mothers attempt to resolve by persuading their child to let go of their favourite toy so the little interloper can have a go. As one American author astringently points out, why should they? Can you blame them for going ballistic? At this age, children have no concept of fair shares or unselfishness; would you relinquish your favourite thing before you're ready to do so, for the sake of appearing to have been brought up properly? It is worth peacefully agreeing: *of course* they can play with it, once baby's moved on to something else, and meanwhile, why not have this one – just to see the look on the other parent's face. Even odder, parents' impeccable manners extend to transference, i.e. rebuking your astonished child for something which the other obnoxious little brat persists in getting up to. Here, 'you' comes in handy, being singular and plural: 'Please can you settle down now, and stop all that noise.'

From three to five, children start forming friendships. What a relief to watch them become more sociable, especially since you make all the arrangements, able to monitor their playmates. At school, goodness knows who their chums will be. What if they fall in with a bad crowd? What if your child is considered to be a bad influence? Sometimes, that isn't your problem (nor hers), but the other family's.

Teasing

When toddlers enter the Age of Reason, they begin to think for themselves and question everything. Testing times, but even when they drive you up the wall, don't make a habit of putting them down. Sarcasm is easy to resort to, and sometimes very funny, except to the child being mocked. Keep going, and the boldest children become withdrawn. Even adults' sense of humour is open to question (especially women's). Just a bit of fun! Many children overreact when teased, but parents often regard it as harmless, 'character-forming' in fact. At home and at playschool, teasing may be different from what goes on at school, but one person's idea of it is another's view of hell: bullying.

There's a fine line here; some experts condemn teasing. It can amuse everybody, but depends on the child herself, taking it as a sign of affection or as evidence of sheer spite. What complicates matters is different moods and circumstances; even different people doing the teasing can affect the reaction. Teasing is unlikely to upset a confident child; if it's unkind, they shrug it off, because being spiteful is the perpetrator's problem. They're the ones making a show of themselves, not the child being teased, particularly when she grins and bears it.

Starting school: be prepared

This can be at the age of four years in the UK although children abroad may not start until six, even seven. It has been advocated that since boys are about 12 months behind girls, they should start a year later. Most parents increasingly set great store by education; don't underestimate children's capacity to learn, depending on how or what they're taught. Early learning goals (for age six) include the following:

- Personal, social and emotional development: confidence to try things; concentrate and sit still; understand what's right and wrong.
- Language and literacy: speak confidently; read familiar words; write name.
- Mathematics: count to ten; recognize numerals and shapes; use terms like 'heavier' and 'lighter'.
- Understanding of the world: ask questions about how things work; find out about environment.
- Physical development: understand what's good for your health and why; control and co-ordinate movement.
- Creative development: recognize patterns (music); explore things like colour and shape.

Starting school is a milestone, not a millstone; approached properly, it avoids the kind of attitude which holds you and your child back. Make the most of any invitations to have a look around and get a good idea of the place by talking to other children and their parents, as well as the teachers. Ignorance isn't bliss, it makes life tricky, so keep up to date with the latest innovations in education. And be prepared for how tired your children are likely to be at first, and how hungry, and how grumpy as a result. Food is fuel, giving us energy; there's no point in forbidding snacks when they get home, even if it is nearly teatime.

Have a couple of practice runs, even when school is within walking distance; judge at what point children need your company. If you're in the habit of providing a taxi service, think on: walking keeps you fit, and starts a child on the way to independence. There'll be times when you need assistance from other parents, for example in setting up a car pool, but this can be made routine early on, giving everybody a break; many schools start children off with half-days, but older siblings are there until the afternoon.

Starting school, to adopt that old cliché, is often the first day of the rest of your lives. Helping your children to make this transition as smoothly as possible gives them the confidence to tackle the other major turning points in their life.

Five to nine, nine to five I: parents at work, children at school (childcare)

The first day at school, the day you rise up, humming the theme to *The Great Escape* or choking back the tears, and not just from trying to hit the high notes in *Without You?* If it's agonizing for parents, imagine how children feel, making their first giant step towards independence. So much time and energy is consumed in ensuring their well-being, it's not easy to adjust, even though we're well aware it's for their own good. But good for us, and time for ourselves, though it's soon swallowed up, rushing back to work.

Childcare

Catch 22: finding decent childcare so parents can go out to work, and earn enough money to pay for decent childcare. The UK is one of the worst countries for childcare provision in Europe; childcare pros and cons are constantly debated, working mothers constantly guilty. It's generally agreed that it should be somebody the child knows well, expert at looking after them, who sticks to a regular routine, providing continuity and security. Under-threes (boys especially) may be better looked after at home, preferably by family members, rather than installed in some form of crèche. Some children thrive on a one-to-one basis, others enjoy being in a group, e.g. a day nursery; they all develop different needs, recreational and educational. Childcare requirements vary according to age, and it can do children a power of good; encouraging social skills from an early age helps them to be more confident.

When choosing somewhere outside the home, call in rather than making an appointment. A swift impromptu visit gives a better idea about what's on offer, judging by the reaction of the person in charge. If first impressions are favourable, arrange to come back and find out more, preferably at the start of the session, to watch the children settling in. Then bring your offspring along for a couple of quick visits before they start 'full-time'. You'll soon know it's the right choice, when the child looks forward to going and keeps talking about what they do.

Requirements checklist
Self
- How much to pay and when; extras: meals, more costs, e.g. travel.
- Flexibility: changes in your job or circumstances.

17

- Cover during holidays and training days (see if your LEA runs supervised activities).
- Cover in event of emergencies, like sudden illness: yours; child's; carer's (back-up for yourself, e.g. swaps with friends and neighbours, and the carer).

Children

- Good relationship: carers and children; co-operation: parents and carers.
- Agreed policy on behaviour and punishments; staff trained for emergency procedures.
- Programme of appropriate and varied activities, including suggestions from the children, who are treated as individuals and allowed to work at their own pace.
- Variety of toys and equipment: books; arts and craft; music; construction toys; jigsaws; sport and games, plus outings and visits for school-age children.

Time management

Doesn't time fly when you're having fun making umpteen arrangements and preparation? Each morning, nightmare on every street, though it's amazing what children can accomplish in ten minutes: washed, dressed, packed, off full speed down the road with a piece of toast jammed in their mouths. Most children could sleep for England, the moment the alarm clock goes off. This, plus one warning from you, should be enough to get themselves up, but no parent risks teacher's bad books. Just one black mark or filthy look should be sufficient to instil a Pavlovian response to the alarm; what a lovely image: buzzzz, and your child sits bolt upright in bed.

Simplify matters by encouraging children to do as much as possible the night before. Yes, they've got tons of work. So have you. Yes, they've no time. Neither have you. Yes, they're worn out. So are you. Who'd do it if you're weren't there? Well, yes, of course, they would, wouldn't they? Nonetheless, many hands make light work, or cause complete and utter chaos, without organizing. Compromise does not equal capitulation: if they're in a mad dash and forgot to do a packed lunch the night before, slap some sandwiches together while they shove their clothes on.

Dressed for success

Problem area for younger children, and not just uniform. Apart from the fun and games of fashion trends, there's the practical side, the nitty gritty of getting the hang of buttons (especially cuffs), fastening ties, doing up laces – distinguishing between left and right. Not to mention learning to be punctual, following directions and obeying instructions. Terrifying on a child's first day, feeling he's the only one in the world who doesn't understand what he's meant to be doing. Since they'll feel more babyish having to ask for help at school, muster your patience and let them learn to dress themselves. It's a boost to their confidence, discovering they can manage; does it matter about loopy laces, as long as they don't come undone?

Even before they can speak, most children know exactly what clothes they want. Some experts insist they must be allowed their way, because any hint of criticism shows you think they're stupid, but say nothing, and when they happily march forth, to be greeted with derision from far less understanding friends and family, who'll be blamed? The great boon of uniform is the avoidance of civil war, though it still causes tussles: the size of heels on shoes; how often a blazer needs washing.

Sam's mum is fed up, sorting out all his uniform. So's he, and there's still some more clothes to buy: once more into the shopping mall. A few hours beforehand, she fetches an old catalogue so he can cut out pictures of the things he wants for school, like stationery, and stick them into a notebook.

Even confident children want their favourite toy with them, but better safe at home rather than risk losing or forgetting them. Everybody is daunted at first by what's new and strange; starting school means children encounter lots of changes, learning to become more independent. They will also have somebody else as a role model. Whether teacher proves an ally or an adversary depends on your self-esteem, as well as your children's.

Five to nine, nine to five II: parents at work, children at home

Successful parent, successful child, and yet your main job is teaching your offspring they don't need you, to get along fine without you. From first encountering the outside world, children start growing away from parents, as well as growing up.

Much-needed support

Once children start school, you may wonder about your role, other than chief cook and bottle-washer, and taxi service. With all the changes in family life: at home, at school, or at work, parents need to continue supporting their children whenever it's required. Reassure them of this; as they grow up, the emotional takes precedence over the practical. Depending on circumstances, they may turn to their friends or other adults, whether a favourite teacher, relative or family friend. But did you automatically confide everything to your parents? Rather than taking it personally, take pleasure in the fact your child has the confidence to seek help, including approaching other adults.

> Melinda's school informs Melanie that her daughter's been caught pinching packets of cigarettes from the corner shop. She dreads telling her husband, and rounds on the girl: 'But why on *earth* didn't you tell me, for heaven's sake? *Why?*' Melinda mutters: 'The clue's in the question, Mother.'

Quality time

The child's world is divided into life at home, with friends, in school, but the degree of overlap means learning more rules and skills. Communication and negotiation or compromise will maintain security, and if you expect their full attention, aim to debate, not dominate, and listen carefully. Children's respect is most easily gained when it's clear how much you respect them; parenting is virtually the opposite of the old saying: 'Never explain, never apologise'. Speaking of useful phrases: 'quality time', coined to assuage working parents' guilt, aims to reserve a special period each day, devoted 100 per cent to your children. Which is when, exactly? The best time for them won't be during their favourite TV show, nor is it convenient for you when late for work, running round scrabbling files and briefcase together. But it is better to make time if it's to your children's advantage, rather than because it happens to suit you, though when they'll need you varies from day to day, even moment to moment.

To be wholly at your children's disposal means they grow up wholly dependent. But when disaster strikes, it feels as if you've spent 24 hours non-stop with them, even if parents and children (particularly teenagers) usually sail around like the proverbial ships that pass in the night. It is damn near impossible juggling work, home, friends, husband, leisure, etc., etc., but try not to let children down by constantly fobbing them off. Insecurity eats away at confidence and lack of attention and poor communication make matters worse. Children have a veritable knack of selecting the worst moment to approach you with something deadly important (and probably say the same of you), but five minutes' undivided attention makes them feel much better. On a regular basis, the improvement in a child with low esteem is almost visible.

When even five minutes is too time-consuming, set a time to talk about it. What about whilst you're making dinner – or rather, while they're helping you in the kitchen? If you're happy with that arrangement, stick to it; messing them about compounds the original problem. Children have to screw up their courage to say anything in the first place; the last thing they need is to feel ten times worse, desperately insecure. We read so often in the daily papers about cases of youngsters running away from home. When a child commits suicide, their family may appear to have no idea why, and doctors have noted suicidal tendencies in children as young as four. It's important to open lines of communication as early as possible, and to keep them open.

Inner and outer confidence

Confidence in ourselves naturally means that we're confident with others. Not necessarily – any more than confidence in what we do is a guarantee of confidence in what we are, or vice versa. You may well hear a teacher's description of your child which is totally at odds with what you know of him, e.g. reserved in the classroom yet boisterous at home. It can easily be the other way round; what a relief when your little imp turns into a cherub at school, or visiting friends' houses. The more confidence a child has, the more easily he can adapt to a different environment, looking forward to the adventure, making the most of the challenge. Better than constantly dreading any changes, even minor ones.

Injecting confidence

Now they're old enough to have a say in the matter, and probably have been for some time, children need their own space; relax with the idea of low maintenance (on both sides) and let them sort out their room so that it's entirely their domain. Encourage them to get used to their own company; there's a big difference between being lonely and enjoying being on your own, and it stands them in good stead. Outside the home, suggest activities they can take part in with other children, anything from acting to aikido; the discipline and the ability to relax involved in hobbies like drama and martial arts do self-esteem the world of good. Keep it within reason, though. Some children persist in trying everything out (or trying it on), expensive in terms of time and energy, as well as money.

Puberty looms: the gender gap; starting secondary school

One damn thing after the other, that's adolescence. Most parents dread it (especially in older age groups), as if all teenagers should have a health warning attached. Many children face the onset of puberty in the last year of primary school rather than the first year of secondary, and while they are undergoing such changes, physically and mentally (in particular, emotionally), it's little wonder self-esteem can suddenly plunge.

The birds and the bees. And blokes

At a remarkably young age, children start asking embarrassing questions, or even laughing at the rude bits in a video before you do. Parent and child may be chock-full of confidence, but that doesn't totally eradicate the embarrassment gene. Many parents are as thrilled as their children at the idea of discussing sex and bodily changes, but if you can't bear to educate them, ensure they know what's what. Remember your own youth – how could you forget? A time of great confusion, half-child, half-adult: more withdrawn; more anti-social; more worry; more embarrassment; more challenges; more partying. That's how most parents sum teenagers up: more, more, more.

State of independence

Parents have an important balancing act: ensuring their offspring's security, whilst helping them prepare for total autonomy. The latter is not a straightforward process, and the more insecure teenagers are, the more it comes about the hard way, forcing separation by means of disagreement. Parents who don't encourage independence are liable to fight back or panic, becoming more clingy, nagging and/or authoritarian. Both sides are prone to go over the top, often resorting to childish behaviour. Adults inclined to discouragement and disparagement may find youngsters respond by deliberately and dangerously seeking thrills; those hell-bent on competing and laying down the law may end up with lazy slobs, with incredible powers of resistance.

Parents cannot resist offering advice, but even the most well-meaning, tactfully worded advice is interpreted as nagging and/or criticism. Of course you know best: you've had the experience, you're qualified to speak, but the bottom line is this sub-text: 'I'm telling you because you can't be trusted to do things properly. You aren't as clever as me, or as good as me, and probably never will be.' Parents

23

would never dream of saying such a thing, but that's what children hear. Simpler to initiate discussion: make suggestions, pointing out implications, possible problems and likely consequences. Pay attention to what they have to say, then, between you, consider the most sensible modifications in order to work it out. Better yet, wait until they ask your advice, or ask them if you can make suggestions.

Gender identity

So much is said about equality, but since we can't all be equal, a better aim is to respect each other's differences. Male and female are very different, but neither is wholly superior to the other. In order to define masculinity, boys have to see themselves as individual and separate, cutting ties with their mothers, which sometimes causes problems with relationships later. By the age of six, they sort of discover their dad, though still needing their mothers (traditionally in the UK, this is the age they are packed off to boarding school). For girls, it's a matter of attachment, hence greater difficulty with being individuals. They're also more observant when it comes to other people's feelings and needs; young men have a more self-centred approach and a desire for action. If they do something wrong, rather than explanations or appealing to their better nature, many parents resort to telling them not to do it again or they'll be punished. Boys' view of morality differs from girls'; the latter appreciate that if you care, you want justice; if you want justice, it shows you care.

As babies, boys are less sensitive to faces nor is their sense of touch as good as girls'. At the toddler stage, boys take up more space, and ignore newcomers to playgroup, whilst girls befriend them. They also need more help with verbal and social skills, outnumbering girls by about four to one with communication problems. Then at school, they cope by attempting to harden their hearts, to cut themselves off from emotions, from fear of tenderness. The resultant stress means they suffer from muscle tension – parents can feel this when they put their arms around them. When girls touch others, their intent is friendly or comforting; boys do it as a means of control. By contrast, at puberty, boys seem to come alive, needing thrills and excitement.

Girls and boys

Teenagers usually hang around in gangs, whether led by music, fashion or computers, but can be roughly divided into two groups: the strong, silent type, i.e. reclusive, the bedroom-hugging, CD-playing, voraciously reading loner; or the party animal. The latter is VERY loud. The two sexes are diverging at this point, but still have in common the power of their vocal cords, shouting and swearing, with girls screeching or giggling. Ah, but boys take up more space, whether sprawling on the sofa or running round grabbing food in the kitchen. Such activity often appears threatening to an onlooker, yet displays of restlessness in boys are said to be an anxiety response. They make less eye-contact, and smile less than girls, yet talk more. Teachers may favour them, offering extra help:

Mr Lawrence: 'That's nice and neat, Julie.'
Julie: 'Thanks, sir.'
Mr Lawrence: 'Not bad, Bob, but if you read the question more carefully (especially that last sentence?), it should give you the right answer.'

Mums and dads

Shy boys may be late developers: career; relationships; marriage. This doesn't appear to be the case with shy girls, though they may go straight from father to husband, not getting a job first (nor while they're married). According to a recent survey, even today, the roles of father and mother are seen as complementary: nurturing and providing, if on the sidelines (despite what might be considered higher status) and at the centre of family life respectively. Children share these views; some are even aware of the problems parents face due to the pressures of consumer culture.

Most fathers seem to feel their job is to ensure all the essentials are available and that their children were well looked after, i.e. materially, which makes life even more frustrating for the low-paid and unemployed. While fathers enjoy the company of their offspring, practicalities have priority: taking them out or taking part in sports; giving them lifts. Few could define 'involvement', but suspect this would put them under too much pressure; such things as caring and communication are left to mothers.

Nonetheless, relationships between teenage girls and their fathers are often affected; uncomfortable with their daughters' burgeoning sexuality, men become withdrawn or authoritarian. Girls fear this kind of rejection, facing a dilemma if parents don't get on. When men pick on their wives, daughters are torn between loyalty to their mother (because they've more in common) and a need for their father's approval.

It's said the main reason so many girls lose their confidence at puberty is the awareness of their role as sexual objects. Girl power?

Many young women believe they should always be nice and kind and put themselves last, anxious to make sure that people like them. Empathy goes overboard; they're more concerned with their friends' needs than their own. At least they get more sympathy where hormones are concerned, e.g. period pains, but for parents it's handy to know that boys' testosterone levels soar by about 800 per cent (more so in a violent environment). No wonder it affects their moods and their energy. When the latter is properly channelled, it's a chief characteristic of leadership, though either for good or for bad. Structure helps boys feel secure. They want to know: what are the rules? Are they fair? Who's the boss?

Starting secondary school

If your offspring's first day at primary school was a big step for you both, children may find secondary school more traumatic. You've got used to not having them around the house, but they need you to be even more understanding, since it coincides with puberty. Confident children realize that their new school has pupils of all shapes and sizes, so there's no reason to feel awkward about the way they're changing. But the trouble with change is that everybody's convinced they're the only one undergoing it: isolated, different from everybody else. Just us, all on our own.

Siblings occasionally help ease the newcomer's initiation, but are more likely to wind them up. You can help, as before, with visits to the school, meeting the teachers, going along to some of the social events. Try and keep in contact, and keep assuring your children there's nothing to worry about. Parents see it as a step forward, but for them, it's all downhill, from the top to the bottom of the heap. And along with having to make new friends, they're probably leaving some of their best friends behind.

Again, decide between you on a flexible routine. Before you know it, they're planning for the future: leaving home or living at home; further education; looking for work.

Young people today: moving up
(university; job) – moving out

Society has long recognized 18 as the age of maturity, as do sensible parents – mostly. Some, though, are so indifferent to their offspring, they leave them to bring themselves up. Or, they're expected to grow up quickly, e.g. children who take care of a parent. Old heads on young shoulders can also be the case in the family of Mr and Mrs Average, if such creatures exist. Many parents do find it difficult to accept their children as mature adults who can manage perfectly well by themselves, thank you.

Home, sweet home

Where children have good jobs, but still live at home, it's usually as well they're at work each day, and spend most of their time out. Sometimes, conflict may not arise as much when students are at home, perhaps because they continue to be dependent on their parents. But an atmosphere of open warfare, or the soul-destroying deadly silence, an uneasy truce at best, does nobody any good, undermining everybody's confidence. Parents are frequently bewildered, not knowing what course of action to take, children are openly resentful. Both are apt to get angry about the slightest thing.

This isn't always a problem, and it never was for centuries when society was made up of adults and adults in miniature: children. They were allowed to be babies until the age of three or four, and then, considered grown-up, were set to work. The twentieth century saw the birth of the teenager (in an American advert for a dress), plus an extraordinary number of changes, metamorphosing from 50s rock 'n' roll to 60s hippy, then 70s punk and glam, followed by 80s new romantic, and the largely retrospective 90s. This alone shows the kind of pressures teenagers come under. Some adults feel young people today have it easy, despite the rising crime rate – and teenage pregnancies, abortions, increased violence, drink and drug problems, the homeless and runaways, health problems, mental health problems.

Never had it so good?

Even for those who manage to escape all or any of the above, the world today seems very complex. Is it worse for girls or for boys? Both are expected to excel in all areas: education, employment, family. Having obtained the necessary qualifications, enough of a hard slog in itself, what then? A first-class job, to which they must devote themselves 100 per cent, then settle down with a family, to which they must also devote themselves 100 per cent. Oh, and leisure time pursuits, which demand 100 per cent devotion. That may be what the future holds, but while living at home, teenagers have all this dinned into them, plus a few variations.

Some families still cannot see the point of education for girls. Sometimes, neither do they: marriage or relationships are the main goals. No matter how emancipated women are believed to be, there's a message constantly coming through via the media: great job, nice home, plentiful friends, wonderful fun in your spare time (in any order), these accomplishments are as nothing, without a boyfriend. How did women grow up to be this insecure?

It's equally confusing for a man, expected to be running a highly successful and demanding career, complemented by an ideal wife and delightful offspring, to whose upbringing he has contributed no less than 50 per cent. How did men have their confidence sapped so that life fails to live up to expectations? Well, even if parents haven't been able to ensure their children are 100 per cent confident, they can still help them to be ready to cope with life's problems next time they pop up, and they always do. Confidence can be instilled at any time while they're growing up (see Part 4).

Prize assets

When it comes to being competitive, many experts feel parents should start intervening early on, i.e. at the toddler stage: in other words, DON'T encourage it because the child's confidence will be fatally undermined. Trouble is (and there will be), it's far worse with teenagers. Now, they are virtually on the same footing as their parents, able to compete on equal terms. This can descend to the ridiculous, clearly shown in TV comedy, with the competitive father who cannot bear to lose going to extraordinary lengths to ensure he always gets the better of his wife and his children.

> Jim's dad is in a good mood, laughing at that show on telly, so Jim decides to ask to borrow the car. 'Why's that then, lad? What's up with that fancy motor of yours? In the garage again? Must be costing you a fortune. I can't afford to be paying out on any damage if you have a bump, not on my wages, I can't.'

And what of daughters, if they're the first one in the family to get the chance to go to university? How many wives shaking their heads, have to spend their lives making compromises, go-between one minute, buffer the next, between spouse and children?

Most of us do have a strong competitive streak, as the overwhelming success of the lottery suggests. Parents tend to get carried away, wanting success for their children sometimes far more than they do themselves: the first baby in the family (in the street, in the town, etc.) to walk and talk. Not that it actually proves anything. Wasn't it Einstein who never spoke in his early years, simply because he had nothing to say? Though imagine a young child having the brain power to reason that one out. But it's generally agreed that it isn't a good idea to overload children with your expectations and crushing their confidence; few of us can get it 100 per cent right the first time every time.

All the same, if there were some way of bottling motivation, it would mean riches beyond comparison. Try a happy medium: praise without pressure, and, equally, comment instead of criticism. All children can achieve things worthy of encouragement. When they slip up, rather than stressing failure, work it out together to see what went wrong and how to avoid it next time. While offering praise whenever the opportunity arises, don't go overboard. Stick to a few kind words; the most colourful picture can be a thing of beauty in itself, but it's unlikely to give Picasso a run for his money. Children soon detect insincerity, and detest feeling embarrassed.

All through their teens, they keep telling you they're NOT children any more. By the time they're 18, your job is done. It's up to them now to make their own decisions, as well as their own mistakes. If they still tend to be obsessed with success and overwhelmed by failure, whenever they encounter problems and need your help and advice, make sure they know you'll still be there to provide support. The best thing you can do is enable them to stand on their own two feet.

Part 2 Family problems (like mother, like daughter; like father, like son); suggestions on tackling them

Families and conflicting opinions

Tolstoy certainly had a point about families, and as another writer recently commented, where would the arts be if there weren't any unhappy families? Logically, parents with good self-esteem have confident children, but it's rather more complicated than that, because, after all, so are families. Many adults hark back nostalgically to their childhood, yet some experts claim that over 50 per cent of children were unhappy growing up; the proliferation of books professing to reveal the secrets of happiness to all those desperately seeking it suggests that not everybody enjoyed an ideal upbringing.

Self-portraits

Since we're all born with good self-esteem, and all it takes to keep it up is plenty of praise and carefully judged constructive criticism, i.e. fair shares of affection and appreciation, what goes wrong? Everybody in the average family also needs a fair dollop of the following: patience; humour; trust; empathy; respect – all mutual.

Self-esteem can become fragile, and when things rise up to beset us, it invariably leads to inner doubts. The majority of people have high expectations of themselves, and when these are unfeasible, cannot avoid questioning their abilities. This is exacerbated by what they imagine are the demands of society: always total success in every area of their lives. So that's what's in store for their children.

'Self-image' is how we picture ourselves, whilst the 'ideal self' is what we fondly imagine we ought to be. When the discrepancy between them becomes a yawning gap, we become anxious, causing self-esteem to plummet. The situation worsens because we are a disappointment to ourselves, and it's clearly obvious to everybody else. We completely lose our sense of proportion, believing that mistakes are always fatal, and failure the end of civilization as we know it.

Accidents will happen

Thus the father whose toddler drops ice cream all over himself and his pushchair is the world's worst parent, incapable of bringing up a child who can behave himself in public. All that's happened is that the poor little thing hasn't yet learned how to handle fiddly things. However, the best means of defence is attack, so the embarrassed parent starts yelling: 'You clumsy idiot! What d'you have to go and do a thing like that for? What a waste!' Indeed, when presenting child with cone, if the parent warns: 'Now, you be careful with that. Don't drop it, whatever you do, or you'll mess up your nice new outfit', guess what? Instead of enjoying the ice cream, the child worries about losing it, and there it goes. Anxiety causes things to go wrong.

It's habit to voice our concerns to avoid mishaps, but invariably, the opposite results, and accidents happen. As a result, the child is immediately and irrevocably labelled 'greedy', 'clumsy', 'stupid'. But what adult can tackle an ice cream without having to wipe their mouth? We clean it off and laugh it off, same as we should with a child. You can't so easily get rid of doubts and fears sown by yelling and name-calling.

Self-confidence is a question of behaviour, whilst self-esteem results from attitude, so changing, or even moderating, the way you behave will have an effect on self-esteem. You buy your child an ice cream for them to enjoy; they don't need encouragement, but by concentrating on saying how good it looks and letting them get on with it means that they're more likely to hang on tight. Saying 'Tuck in!' is more positive than 'You're going to drop it if you're not careful.'

As children become aware of their mental and physical qualities, self-esteem begins to form. Tell them they're bright as a button, and they shine; marvel how well they dance or draw, and they try and do even better. With criticism, beware the self-fulfilling prophecy, because it proves lethally effective. Parents congratulate themselves on how well their children have done, but when everything starts going wrong, somebody has to take the blame. Both child and parent may end up full of guilt, though some adults insist their offspring are entirely at fault, or blame their friends. Over-protective parents either refuse to admit anything is wrong or assume total responsibility. Meanwhile, over-competitive parents puzzle about how come that early promise fizzled out, whilst those with little confidence sadly reflect on their offspring's constant failures. Nonetheless, many teenage tearaways are highly successful as adults, and many a child who was good as gold goes off the rails.

Nagging pain

Until the age of seven, children don't usually question their parents' judgement. They obey in order to please them, being too young to understand why they have to do certain things. The onus is on us to be as fair as possible; accidents shouldn't be regarded as bad behaviour or disobedience. Parents often fail to realize how often they're critical, never mind the occasional tirade, about, say, poor school reports. Our words prey on a child's mind, morning, noon and night, especially if accompanied by threatening gestures; to small children, annoyed adults loom extremely large:

> 'Hurry up and get your breakfast down you! And *don't* leave a mess like that!'

> 'Get to bed *now*! After putting up with you all day, I'm entitled to a bit of peace.'

Of course we're not that harsh the whole time, and after all, it's only because we're tired or fed up. Some parents are continually on their children's backs, even when it isn't justified. Once something's habit, we don't really notice. Children do. Each time, they're absorbing this message: they're useless, worthless, nothing but trouble. Most parents would protest: 'But that's not what I said at all!' Indeed not, but that's what they think you mean. Ultimately, it's what they'll believe to be true.

Standing in somebody else's shoes

Low self-esteem means you take everything personally, forever needing to justify yourself, to avoid responsibility, like the celebrity who appealed to a talk show host: 'I'm NOT defensive. I'm not, am I, Victoria? Am I?' To have a good self-image means to be yourself and to accept yourself, good and bad, and, consequently, helps you to be accepting of other people. Being able to empathize with others improves relationships. With your children, think back to your younger days, not just your most embarrassing moments, full of resentment when you were unfairly blamed, but how brilliant it felt when you were doing something exciting.

Give children credit where it's due, but discriminate: too much praise, too easily, places less value on what they've worked hardest at to accomplish. By contrast, too much criticism is lethal, killing off self-esteem, so that many children become bullies or bullied. Figures also show that families where parents are either over-protective or neglectful tend to produce bullies. Or children who end up being bullied.

Picking up on the pecking order

According to one pessimistic viewpoint, people are more likely to get angry in family life than in any other situation. Yet many of us rush into marriage, all bright white hopes and rosy tints, and as for a family: how many children? Boys or girls? That looks like being resolved in the near future, although in China, where families are allowed only one child and have traditionally favoured sons, currently a whole generation of 'little lords' is being raised, with few brides to suit them.

Getting picked on

Family relationships are complex: mother and father; parent and child; siblings. Within each of these, and as a whole, a pecking order applies; at worst, one person becomes the scapegoat: forever ill or having accidents, getting into trouble, and always blamed for everything. Or for being a bit of an individual.

Many families see themselves as a unit; things are 'just so', or done in a certain way 'because they always have been'. Woe betide the odd one out who won't toe the line or wants to try something different. Disastrous for self-esteem, especially as siblings invariably side with their parents. When such children resort to attention-seeking, it incurs more rejection, so they're rarely able to form satisfactory relationships as adults. However, research shows that those who do have families often make successful parents, perhaps by reversing the way they were treated as children.

Intelligent thinking

When it comes to IQ, mother invariably comes bottom, according to both daughters and sons. The latter usually think their IQ is higher than their father's; women tend to set theirs lower. They are also assumed to have a lower IQ, although recent findings suggest that intellectual ability is inherited via mothers. Nonetheless, adult men are often patronizing about them, which is believed to result from resentment, because their earlier intimacy made them vulnerable. There's an ancient joke about women being almost totally responsible for looking after their sons in their formative years, then moaning about the way they turn out. But it's said that men grow up to dislike or be wary of women as a result of the treatment they received as children, particularly if constantly humiliated in front of their peers. Fear and resentment of their mother turn to anger and hate, directed at other women.

33

Along with sibling rivalry, gender provokes complaints: boys reckon sisters have it easy; girls insist boys get away with murder. Currently, it's held that feminism has triumphed; it's a girl's world, and most parents want daughters. But in some families, a child of the wrong sex is seen as a disaster. Likewise, the one whose looks are different. When continually made conscious of things like this, they're bound to lose confidence. Cinderella and the Ugly Sisters are still going strong, aided and abetted by parents who persist in making comparisons: Beauty and the Beast; brains and brawn. Ideally, children should be treated as individuals, their particular talents recognized.

Parent and child reunion

As children grow up and their mates call round, parents develop a curious habit, sort of 'making their presence felt': Dad answering the phone and telling jokes while son clambers out of the shower.

> Katie's in the kitchen, making coffee for her three closest friends, when her Mum pops her head round the door to see if anyone fancies some biscuits. 'No, thank you, Mrs Bradshaw,' they chorus politely. But in she comes, and starts fishing out packets of this and that. Still no takers, and now she's on about the dangers of dieting.

Whether parents are overly self-effacing or kidding themselves they're one of the crowd, children can't wait for them to clear off. Some adults can't seem to resist this kind of role play: 'Look, I'm still a part of your life, even if you are all grown-up now'. It's like the way toddlers tug at your clothing when you chat to your friends. The actions of parent and child mirror each other, yet both resent what the other does.

Until daughters are settled with families of their own, round about their 30s, they aren't always the best of friends with their mothers. In fact, mothers may feel they're the ones at a disadvantage, and worry about falling out with their daughters. This seems pessimistic since many relationships become steadier once adolescence has been safely negotiated. Women in their 50s and 60s don't always seem comfortable with their mothers, but generally, the situation appears to be improving, despite (or because of?) this century's reversal from housewife and mother to working mother.

As for fathers and daughters, according to an interesting piece of research about gender and argument, not one parent reported a falling out, and the children cited only a few instances, usually about anger.

Those who said they were afraid of their father appear to have suffered in silence. One conclusion was that daughters feared that a serious argument would affect the whole family. Conflict between father and son can sometimes bring this situation about, with the mother forced to choose between them.

Problems also arise from the gap between the generations and the clash of personalities, described, simplistically, as introverts versus extroverts; the former regarded with suspicion as 'too deep', the latter dismissed as 'so shallow'. The parent who was an only child is often perplexed by his sizeable brood, likewise the parent from a large family taking care of one scion. Pros and cons for big families and singletons are many and varied, but coming from one to the other takes adjustment. If your background was gregarious, how do you cope with a loner? And only children as parents are bemused by the fierce rivalry and equally fierce loyalty of siblings.

Family planning

Research shows that it's the number of children as well as when you have them which can affect confidence. With larger gaps between children, there are often fewer demands, so parents are more relaxed. Consequently, when there are one to three years between siblings, they don't seem to get on as well with their parents as those where there's a gap of one to five years. In some large families where children are born close together, thus receiving less attention from their parents (or they're dictatorial), there's a tendency towards lawlessness, but children may also turn out entrepreneurial.

As for intelligence, although the youngest child has the advantage of more intellectual interaction, their IQ is likely to be lower. Similarly, only children, whereas older children learn more, probably through being in a position to teach their younger siblings. Siblings born less than two years apart are more likely to drop out of education, although in general, they are happier than those where the gap is over two years. Here, because of the greater opportunity to be the centre of parents' attention, it leads to rivalry; siblings are often overshadowed by their elders, but the bigger the gap, the more they'll compete. For older children, it's the other way round; they're more ambitious to do better than those who are closest in ability; they bother less when there are more years between them, being used to coming out on top.

Singletons and siblings

Only children are either envied or pitied, as likely to be extremely sure of themselves (to the point of arrogance or bossiness) when they have benefited from their parents' undivided attention, as to be spoilt rotten. Parents should encourage their offspring to invite friends round; it can be hard for them to relate to other children. Spending more time in adult company either rubs off to make them seem mature, or the extra attention makes them more of a brat. They are also likely to be perfectionists, inflexible and controlling, consequently prone to anxiety. This can also apply to the eldest child, presumably because first-time parents may transmit their own worries.

By the time it comes to the youngest child, some parents grow neglectful, leaving siblings to bring them up, whilst others spoil them rotten. Such youngsters don't have much chance to learn responsibility when there's always somebody else to do things for them. As for poor piggy in the middle, what chance do they have? Neither indulged like the baby, nor allowed to do what the eldest gets away with, they're too old to put up with the one and too young to hang around with the other. But the middle child often makes friends more easily, and may get on best with siblings.

Two or four children can make for a balance, though rivalry seems as likely. Gender complicates the situation with three children; when the eldest is a girl, she may take on a mothering role, while a boy may have to take charge. There's often a romantic view of large families, i.e. five or more (many more) children: fewer possessions but richer affection and better relationships with everybody helping look after everybody else. Most problems, though, can be resolved, or avoided, when parents first come home with the new baby. The more the older child is encouraged to help take care with younger siblings, the better the chance of building up a good relationship, and the confidence of all the children remains intact.

Common problems with young children I

Self-confidence is invariably affected by conflict between parent and child, and disagreements being verbal, at the toddler stage, things can go rapidly downhill. This often happens when, instead of being guided by the stages of development, parents go by the progress of the most precocious youngster around, fretting that their offspring lags behind. But the average child doesn't turn up for the first day of school clad in nappies, bottle gripped in paw.

Of the three key areas at this stage in a child's life: sleeping, eating and toilet training, all seem equally traumatic. Being tired causes bad temper, in itself leading to problems elsewhere. Still, whilst all parents recall the early struggles, mostly children don't, although some develop habits which cause great problems, such as eating disorders. The constant battle of wills wears down self-esteem, and when both parent and child have low self-esteem, it leads to constant fighting. Bad eating and sleeping habits make you feel lousy and result in rows, rows affect confidence . . . round and round we go. Vicious circles need to be broken, before such links are forged.

Golden slumbers

A good night's sleep does wonders for us; weariness makes us feel awful, all the time. Yes, everyone knows that having babies is a tiring business (one advice book cheerily points out that nobody ever died from lack of sleep), but it still causes horrendous problems. Along with coping with our own exhaustion, how much more energy is depleted in the hours and hours spent trying to persuade children to go to sleep?

Obviously, some need more sleep than others. In one household, you could have a child with enviably normal sleeping patterns, one who would hibernate given half a chance, and another who gets by on a few hours each night, catching up with the odd bout of a solid 12 hours. And which is harder for parents, getting children up in time or getting them to bed on time? Both are exceptionally stressful, for all the many ingenious tricks of the trade. One useful point of view is that insomnia gives you more time to get things done; 'twas Napoleon who dismissed the fabled eight-hour sleep as being 'for fools', though generously allowing a whole six hours for the ladies.

By definition, a 'good' baby sleeps like he invented it, not a peep out of him all night long. But most babies need feeding at least once overnight; in theory, bottle-feeding wins on points, since it means fathers can do fair shares on the night shift (difficult to type with a straight face). Once fed, changed and cuddled, and still wide awake, what then? As mentioned earlier, it isn't a good idea to respond immediately to outraged howls; babies need time to settle down. But it seems much harder to cope with a baby who will not sleep when you're dying to get to bed, rather than one who doesn't fancy eating, let alone learning to do without a nappy. The thought that he will cry himself to sleep, eventually, through sheer exhaustion, is not always borne out by reality; sometimes it's the exhausted parent who falls asleep, waking, usually, to blissful silence.

Cat naps (dog-tired)

Babies, after all, have more opportunity to snooze, lulled off when out in their buggy or pram or in the car. In extreme cases, taking babies out for midnight walks gives you fresh air and exercise, and helps keep you going. Some parents adapt, catching up on beauty sleep by taking an afternoon nap with their offspring. Reserving this time to relax is a sensible way to boost energy levels. Besides, although babies can howl like banshees, they can't pester the life out of you. Toddlers soon learn the power of speech: what I want, I will get in the end.

Time for bed

Before children get that far, teach them that you mean what you say. Avoid bedroom brawls by making it clear you won't respond to attempts at attention-seeking. Delete 'just this once' from your daily vocabulary, and reserve it for a special treat. Stick to a night-time routine: bath and bedtime story or chat, then lights down. The bedroom should be a haven, not a cell. There's no harm in leaving a child to his own devices if he wants to look at a book or listen to a cassette, something to settle him down. TV, video or computer are often regarded as first-class babysitters (and can sometimes be a boon for busy parents), but in the bedroom, with unlimited access, they provide undue stimulation. Yes, they keep children quiet for hours, and wide awake. At least when they start school, for the first few weeks, weariness makes them go out like a light.

Common problems with young children II

It may be obvious that we are what we eat, but nobody is entirely certain what they're eating. Time was when freshly baked scones were inedible by the following day, fizzy drinks, once opened, soon went flat. And take water, which we're meant to swallow by the gallon every day (speaking as someone who carted a litre bottle around with her first-born). If so, which is better: bottled or straight from the tap? No wonder parents panic, battling every day with the tyranny of choice, racking their brains about what to buy, before even contemplating the best nourishment for children.

Nutritionally speaking

From the start, there's a dilemma: bottle or breast; whatever method, you soon know whether you have a fussy eater. Each stage is ripe for conflict: moving on to solids; learning to feed themselves; choosing their own food and learning to cook. Toilet training is a relatively short episode, bedtime comes but once a day, but feeding is on a collision course. For new parents, correct nourishment for the baby is of paramount importance. Bottle-feeding is considered more convenient (plus you can tell how much the baby's taken); breast may be more nutritious, providing the mother is careful with her diet. Few parents worry whether a bonny baby is headed for a life-time of large-scale misery, but they always fret that she's not putting enough weight on.

> Aileen's new baby barely seems to take any milk at all, and persists in falling asleep after a few minutes, even when the nurses try keeping him awake by tickling him. She's amazed to learn that the test weigh shows that, compared to the average baby, he's guzzling down twice as much in half the time.

By contrast, you could start off with a child so fussy, she once needed ten feeds in one day, and grew up to be petite, but eats like a horse. But all children have different eating habits, and tastes, as you discover, moving on to solids. Ideally, we'd all eat when we are hungry and stop when we're full, and eat foods, naturally, which are good for us. Left to themselves, the first part is what most children would do, whilst the second is up to us, trying to ensure they get proper meals. A child's idea of a balanced diet tends to be a soft drink in one hand and a plate of burger and fries in the other.

Feeding fiascos

Weaning can make life easier for babies who didn't take to a liquid diet, but should proceed at their pace, especially with them deriving comfort as well as nourishment from being breast- or bottle-fed. Introducing solids can be tricky when parents have varying ideas about nutrition, from experts on macrobiotics to junk food junkies. As far as any new parent is concerned, if a child won't eat, then she will surely die, right now, right in front of us.

No wonder we get into a flap, rather than assuming, well, maybe she isn't hungry right now, so we'll try again later. For years, the correct feeding routine for babies was rigidly set at four-hour intervals, and they had to wait, even if they howled the place down. Then the turnaround: feeding on demand (and goodness, are some babies demanding), allowing for a little embellishment, i.e. calculating how late on the last feed could be, to grab a few hours sleep before the next one.

Stuffing yourself until you're bursting makes you feel horrendous, while any food eaten when you really are hungry is delicious, though few people let themselves get that famished. Babies feed when they're hungry, and even when awkward, can't do it on purpose. However, because toddlers ultimately have to toe the line in most areas, for once, mealtime puts them in control. Any anger or resentment or fear is easily expressed by the refusal to try even one mouthful. The most confident parents may find it impossible to stay relaxed, reduced to desperation with a child who won't eat, or eats only what suits them. Once this is a regular state of affairs, the child may begin to refuse to eat even when hungry.

Poor eating habits can escalate into a huge problem. There isn't a parent alive who hasn't had experience of breakfast battlefields or suppertime strife – it's amazing that ALL adults aren't affected. Food is nourishment, and one of life's greatest pleasures; these days, cookery is virtually the eighth art, yet increasing numbers of people suffer from food allergies and eating disorders. Like many problems which beset teenagers especially, it's invariably caused by low self-esteem.

Toilet training

What's the last thing most women do before leaving the house, and the first thing upon entering another establishment, such as a restaurant? Visit the toilet, and locate it, respectively. The fact that facilities for women are invariably inadequate compared with gentlemen's isn't the only reason why there are always lengthy queues. Could it have something to do with rigorous toilet training as a child? And how come when the need arises in a public place to visit the toilet, women tend to excuse themselves whilst men announce where they're going?

Finally disposing of nappies is the milestone most welcomed by parents, but training children to use a potty usually makes for a stressful situation because they're mortified if a child has an accident. That degree of embarrassment convinces children they've been naughty, and they suffer accordingly. Just imagine being on holiday, wandering around, child in arms, and suddenly realizing that the fastenings of their plastic pants are gaping, and they've sprung a leak, all over the carpet at Sandringham Palace. Like most horrendous childhood incidents, time turns it into an anecdote.

Instead of being thankful for the greater convenience when children are toilet trained – no more changing or washing of nappies – parents often treat the process as a matter of great urgency (and secrecy), undertaking it with military precision. One expert used to recommend devoting an entire day to the exercise, you and your little one holed up in the kitchen, surrounded by packets of crisps and huge quantities of water. And a potty. Get clean quick schemes are not ideal, even if every other child you know the same age (and even younger) than yours is clean and dry.

The child herself provides the best guide for this stage of development. When you change her nappy and discover it's dry, that's the first sign she's learning control. Once it's dry after being on overnight, you're on the right track, but let nature take its course. Have the potty to hand so the child gets used to the idea, but don't plonk her on by the minute or make her stay there until she performs. Before you know it, she'll be asking for the potty or to go to the toilet, usually at the top of her voice in the poshest of gatherings. And watch out when taking children to the ladies: they have a knack of flinging the door open right in the middle, or getting you locked in. No wonder many adults are obsessed with the state of their bowels and affected with constipation or diarrhoea; both are frequently symptoms of stress.

Difficult children I: red rag to a bull

Whenever children behave atrociously, nobody will believe any of their parents' excuses. However, all naughty children are difficult – but not all difficult children are naughty. Most parents reading this after yet another head-to-head with a tiresome toddler or troublesome teenager assume that 'difficult' is synonymous with 'naughty' (and that first syllable's spelt 'sin'). A no-win situation as far as parents, children and self-confidence are concerned. Children who are continually upset and behave so badly that they constantly upset their parents, are unlikely to receive the treatment they need, which would help their self-esteem.

Parents soon know all right when they have a difficult baby: unbelievably loud, restless, fussy, cranky. Nothing seems to please him, nor settle him: always problems with feeding and sleeping, and ten times worse when introducing changes or something new. The usual conclusion is colic, which is an extremely painful complaint. However, it may be blameless, though it appears to be doctor's favourite diagnosis when you visit the surgery yet again, exhausted and frustrated due to your child's constant distress.

Temper, temper

At times, it seems yours must be the naughtiest child in the world, let alone the street or school. However, it has been estimated that about one-fifth of children should be classed as 'difficult', the term used for those who display the characteristics described below, i.e. due to their temperament. Such traits may also manifest temporarily, when they are at an awkward age, as it were, or facing major changes: serious illness, parents divorcing, moving house, changing school. The term does not apply to youngsters diagnosed with syndromes: autism, attention deficit disorder, hyperactivity, oppositional defiant disorder.

On realizing they've got a difficult child on their hands, most parents ask themselves, 'What have I done to deserve this?' The usual answer is nothing. Nurture and environment have an effect, specifically certain situations and settings, but basically, it's innate. Sheer naughtiness is one thing, but when a child's temperament results in constant over-reaction to something upsetting, parents should concentrate on the way that the child is behaving, in other words, how, not why, and what they can do to contain it.

Some experts identify several different types, but the chief characteristics seem to fall into two distinct groups (not as simple as introverts and extroverts): loud, easily over-excited children, who are exceptionally active; stubborn; disruptive; impulsive; unpredictable. Or, quiet, easily overwhelmed children: unusually dreamy; passive; sensitive; obstinate; clingy; fussy. To complicate matters, both types can also find it hard to adapt, resisting change and anything new, and often exhibit more than one characteristic. Although some traits appear complete opposites, they may overlap at times, resulting in behaviour which baffles parents even more.

Nicky can never sit still to watch TV, even his favourite programme, but give him paper and paints and he works away for hours. Then his mum can't get him to stop.

Sweet reason?

Knowing that your child may be difficult but he is normal comes as a relief, and it makes matters a little easier, recognizing that he's not deliberately misbehaving. Allowances should also be made, e.g. for clumsiness, when youngsters haven't acquired the necessary skills. But there always has to be a reason as far as adults are concerned, even if they can't fathom out what. When parents have low self-esteem, they assume the child's motive must be to deliberately upset them. If behaviour is due to temperament, they can stop feeling bothered and bewildered and guilty, and start working out the best way to cope.

Repeated behaviour results in the same response: i.e. over-reacting or inconsistency, and leads to ineffectual discipline and bad habits, in both parent and child. They're stuck with it. Parents assume the answer must be more discipline, disregarding the fact that whatever they've been doing doesn't work. Easing up is often regarded as giving in or giving up. Still, a relaxed atmosphere works wonders in most situations, as does patience. Even if convinced nothing will work, rather than worrying, concentrate on finding an effective strategy. It's important for child and parents, and the rest of the family, school and neighbourhood.

Speaking of family, don't overlook siblings. Either they start playing up, or take on their parents' worries, trying to be good as gold. But perfect children are liable to grow up to be adults with problems. If they are old enough to understand, explain why the other child gets what looks like special treatment. Besides, since more is expected of 'easier' children, i.e. maturity and independence, they also deserve treats. Ironic that parenting is what you learn from your children, and that parents set such store by their expectations of the child, when he's likely to set his heart on the complete opposite.

Difficult children II: some strategies

Basic good manners and reasonable behaviour result from good discipline, and that requires consistency, clarity, calmness, assertion, authority. One recommended strategy for helping difficult children is to set apart a quiet week (covering most situations) to identify traits and assess the degree of difficulty, e.g. marks out of ten: selfish; complaining; impulsive; rude; intrusive; disruptive; defiant. Make notes and discuss, calmly, with your partner, e.g. what effect is this having on family and friends? Consider several solutions, and any variations. Match behaviour with setting and situation. Plus frequency, from daily routine to encountering strangers. How did she react? Children with low self-esteem can be exceptionally negative, sabotaging treats.

> Emma and Jane's mum is taking them to choose some Christmas presents and then they'll go for a meal. Emma insists that none of the party frocks she's shown would suit her, and at the restaurant, can't eat because of a sudden stomachache.

Tackling the main problems

The time has come to draw the line, the list of what must be dealt with. Based on all your information, discard what can be ignored, concentrating on four to six problems. Minor annoyances may be easier to solve, once others are successfully dealt with. Swap with your partner and start again, to agree on a policy and support each other. Parents become wary of difficult children, if not terrified, but an attitude of 'anything for a quiet life' hands them inordinate power. For example, if a child is persistently intrusive, that's a priority because everybody is entitled to some privacy, and should respect others. Compromise, giving up one thing in order to keep something else, making it their choice, where possible, rather than your decision.

Good discipline is laying down the law, not laying into your children. Often, punishment handed out in the heat of the moment is also inappropriate. Wait until you calm down, then discuss it. Don't assume the child knows what's what; explain simply what you expect, and what will happen if they misbehave. Always follow it up. One warning is fair enough, because we all make mistakes, then stick to your guns. Don't get drawn into arguing, coaxing or making threats.

Offering rewards

If attempts at discipline have failed until now, it's hard to believe anything will work, but difficult children need structure and consistency. Set a good example; they can hardly settle, if you're so disorganized you dive round like a scalded cat every morning. Encourage them to decide their own routine (e.g. breakfast first, or getting dressed?), with things like visual reminders, e.g. a chart decorated with stickers to help. Those with the trait of persistence acquire good habits, while the sensitive are reassured by routine. Negative children are hard to deal with (so much for romantic heroes being aloof and distant), and parents are prone to feeling underappreciated, but any progress should still be rewarded with praise and occasional recompense, like staying up at the weekend to watch a video. Avoid bribery; rewards come after a job well done.

When promising treats, choose something specific, allowing them a say, or use a points system to earn them. Something realistic; we're not talking about a pony for Christmas, and children love little goodies. Speaking of which, don't expect saintly behaviour for a solid six months; if they've managed six or seven times out of the last ten, they're getting the hang of it. Make big tasks easier, by letting them have a go bit by bit; if you tidy their room by shoving everything into the wardrobe, let them tackle one cupboard at a time. Once the new system looks promising – reward yourself.

Punishing schedule

When anticipating tricky situations, one warning should suffice, just beforehand, not miles in advance, or repeatedly, or with long, involved explanations. Show you mean business, no shrugging or apologetic smiles, conveyed with a deadly serious tone. Once children start adapting their behaviour, key words should then have the desired effect, e.g. 'Steady on' to a boisterous child. Ah, the good old days when your parents told you how one look from their parents guaranteed instant obedience. After you've explained, if you still get 'But why?' one expert allows you the old favourite 'Because I say so.' Simpler still: 'That's the rule.'

Punishment should be short and simple, but don't get emotional, especially when assessing whether the child's bad behaviour is due to temperament. If so, he can't help himself, and your response is sympathy to calm him down. But when he's naughty, punishment should be applicable, at home and abroad as it were, denial of privileges or treat: missing a favourite TV programme, or no sweets from the supermarket. You know what your child hates to miss out on, so the list needn't be extensive; one little girl whose lovely golden locks were washed daily would be angelic rather than wait 48 hours.

More importantly, the child learns a sense of responsibility, since the choice is left to him: behave or be punished. Useful for most children, not that they'll give in graciously (would you?), but they learn to obey. If he makes a show of you in public, don't humiliate him, to try and gain control, or to get your own back.

Helping children to help themselves

By the age of three, used carefully, labels can enable children to understand their particular temperament, in order to manage it. Describe actions, rather than your reaction: 'I expect you're fed up by now', not 'You make me so annoyed the way you always keep on fidgeting!'

From four to five, children begin to see that their behaviour is due to temperament, not because they're bad or wrong. They should also understand about taking responsibility and not making excuses. As they learn to deal with it, by calming down, having more patience, 'changing' their mind (i.e. thinking more positively), each achievement is one more step to improving confidence.

Trouble spots

(See pp. 48–51 for problems affecting quiet children.)

Over-excitement

Watch for signs, without being hawk-eyed, to prevent any trouble; allow for the fact that nothing is sure to work every time.

Help the child to let off steam: dance, or run around outside if he's been cooped up or cool down with something absorbing (sand and water play, cuddles, books, video). Create a particular place to go to at home; also useful when he has a tantrum.

Distraction: helping you with simple tasks or making a snack. Paying him extra attention seems odd if you feel it's rewarding him for bad behaviour. But you're not giving in to him, nor giving him what he wants; the reward is for making an effort to calm down.

Irregularity

While sticking to set times for meals and for bed, you cannot force a child to eat when he isn't hungry nor sleep when he isn't tired. Keep mealtime routine flexible enough to suit everybody, but don't be making him special meals whenever he wants.

Tommy ate most of his breakfast this time, but says 'no' to everything his mum suggests for lunch. She hands him a dinner plate so he can collect what food he wants, bargaining so there's a balance between that and things which are nourishing. He's encouraged to help with preparation, and shown how to work the microwave.

Restlessness

It's detrimental to children when they can't focus and teachers everywhere will bless you for solving this. Impulsive children need close supervision or they will constantly disrupt everyone else. They may need time out to break the cycle (treat or task); if ten minutes at meals is the longest they can sit still, let them leave the table.

Practising what you preach

Parents need to be in the right frame of mind to deal with each situation, stepping back or avoiding something when they aren't calm enough. Once they see there is a pattern, forewarned is forearmed, working out the best way to react to a situation, and planning to avoid future confrontations. The latter is better for coping with irregular behaviour; when parents are taken offguard, they can't react appropriately.

When the child's behaviour is assessed as arising from temperament, it's managed firmly but sympathetically. If he's deliberately naughty, parents can ignore it or make a minimal response, using a stern tone of voice: 'That's enough!' One warning is usually sufficient, then the threatened punishment is applied, intended to help the child understand the error of his ways, not make him suffer. Sending him to his room or cancelling any treat is simple and effective. Try not to relent (well, not every single time), or he'll continue to get away with murder, affecting everybody's confidence.

Difficult children III: shrinking violets; more strategies

Shyness is seen as the main characteristic of sensitive children, and it contributes to low self-esteem, whilst low self-esteem causes shyness. In the USA, it's recognized as a treatable psychiatric disease, 'social phobia', affecting one in eight people.

Shy children are often perceived as dear little things, but life is hard for shy adults: passive; not knowing how to speak up for themselves or ask for help; feeling inferior; lacking the opportunity to improve social skills; always worrying about failure or rejection; easily upset; fearful about encountering anything new.

Touchy subject

In children, toys and clothes take getting used to, while for babies, even baths can be frightening. It's heartbreaking for parents when a baby doesn't like being cuddled. Some are so sensitive, being rocked over-stimulates them; they are literally smothered by affection. Hard to imagine that degree of discomfort in our touchy-feely society:

> Distant cousin Fred has arrived, and though you're well over 21 now, he sweeps you off your feet. A huge, bewhiskered, noisy stranger, hugging you fit to burst, he keeps plonking beery, smoky kisses all over your face.

With babies, find a tactful way of warning family members not to terrify them: look don't touch, rather than set the newcomer's five senses all quivering. Parents should remain calm, seeking clues: whatever soothes the baby should become routine. Avoid noisy or brightly coloured toys, although favourites come in useful for many roles. Big, furry animals look after the child at night-time or when he's ill; cuddly toys keep secrets (telling problems to 'worry dolls' last thing helps you wake up feeling tons better); dolls or action figures might be sensitive, so the child becomes their mentor, reinforcing what he's learnt about managing temperament (who says Barbie doesn't have problems?).

Shying away

The problems with attention-seeking children also apply to those who are sensitive – though the last thing they need is to attract attention. Many events are enlivened by party animals, who confess (after several drinks) that they're shy, really. Loud behaviour in children often covers up shyness, whilst quiet children may have ample confidence. Shy parents often have shy children; extrovert parents dub theirs shy because of opposing natures, taken aback or alarmed when their quiet offspring enjoys the company of a few close friends rather than popularity. Some parents encourage children to think of themselves as shy because it's an instant excuse for anti-social behaviour. And sensitivity is the legendary sign of an artistic temperament.

If it is likely to be a problem, children exhibit signs before the usual 9–18 months phase, and take longer to get over it. Any situation affecting security can make the most confident person shy, if temporarily, e.g. moving house, serious illness. But allowing shy children to stay home through constantly 'not feeling well' may develop into school phobia. A quiet word with teachers, and other adults he's in contact with, is not ensuring an easy ride but setting up a consistent way of dealing with the situation. Here, the 'kid gloves treatment' school of thought and 'throwing them in at the deep end' face up to each other; extremes can be disastrous.

Sensitive treatment

Shyness is not a fault, and parents should appreciate this, making sure that children do too; they can learn to cope, particularly when more assertive. If he's withdrawn, he'll find it hard enough talking to you, so don't dismiss or belittle attempts at explaining his feelings. It takes patience and practice to strike a balance between being a shield and being supportive. Be realistic but optimistic, avoiding negative comments or grumbling about things being wasted because of a refusal to participate. The shy child is not one for surprises, no matter how nice parents think they are; get him used to the pleasure of anticipation. Smooth their path with as much preparation as possible. They usually progress when allowed to go at their own pace, providing you avoid making comparisons. Introduce things bit by bit: once he's unwrapped the new toy so desperately desired and which he now shows no interest in, leave it where he can see it until he's used to it. The fashionable new T-shirt? Leave it hanging in the wardrobe, even if it ends up under a jumper to keep him warm in winter.

Trouble spots

Over-sensitive

Life is not a bed of roses, but some people see nothing but thorny problems. Parents should make allowances for more delicate off-spring, not to let them off the hook but so they can make the most of things. Such children need to be encouraged to understand their temperament, and learn how to be comfortable with themselves.

Obsessive

Highly problematic, it's important not to let this kind of behaviour get out of hand; put a stop to it rather than constantly trying to explain, reason or negotiate. When something isn't 'right', a child feels compelled to do things over and over, or makes you do them, but ends up having a tantrum, because it's never going to feel right. Give them clear warning that you'll do it again, then they have to put up with it. You've nothing to lose; they just have the tantrum sooner, so better to concentrate on sorting that out than waste time repeating yourself. Where possible, circumvent; if they loathe the feeling of being buttoned-up, try other fastenings. Let them choose, to avoid a continuing protest, but make it two clear choices because they'll agonize over decisions in case they're 'wrong'.

Change

When something different is about to happen, simple explanations should give shy children an idea of what to expect, rather than warning them off. Repetition and too much detail are classic signs of anxiety, which children can always sense. Familiarity eases out fear, but few people are instantly at ease when first doing something, or in groups of strangers. Experiences can continue to be as scary as the first time for shy children; think back to those hideous ordeals you anticipated: the teenager's party where you hardly knew anybody, but SHE said she might be there.

Empathy is vital, but some of us have high maintenance toleration compared with others; one person's eeensy weensy spider is another's tarantula. Consider the reaction and depth of emotion, not the trigger. Don't let the child's reaction bother you, but continue to be supportive; many adults hate change, and it's rarely as cataclysmic to them as it appears to be to children. With everyday things, when they have trouble adapting, being able to tell the time can teach them flexibility; use a big toy clock so they clearly see how long they've got. This helps them get the hang of switching from one thing to another, e.g. tidying toys up before getting ready for bed.

Whining

We all do it, but a whingeing child can be a pain. Distraction is the best bet, though negative children seem downright impossible to please. Sadly, this is their problem and they have to learn to deal with it. Don't take it personally or feel guilty because they're rarely satisfied. Remain neutral, riding it out rather than attempting to jolly them up or placate them; bribery is asking for trouble.

Inattentive

It's pleasant daydreaming, but some children live in a world of their own. No matter how often you repeat things, they're too absorbed to hear, and shouldn't be punished for ignoring you. Make certain they pay attention: maintain eye contact, dropping down to their level, e.g. sitting on the arm of the chair (and putting the TV on hold); hold their hand, or touch them on the arm or shoulder, speaking simply and clearly.

Optimistic outlook

When shy children have a particular talent, plenty of praise should coax them out of their shell. Encouragement is a good means of distraction, and they may even forget themselves and become more outgoing. Similarly with hobbies and activities; if they enjoy writing and drawing, the subjects they choose give you some idea of what's going on in their head. Older children may find drama useful, or at least role play, rehearsing so they feel more confident, for example, answering the telephone.

Shy children are often so easily overwhelmed that their initial response to anything new is to cling or cringe, refuse to talk, or burst into tears. Forcing them to get on with it means tantrums, from fear, as much as anger, paving the way for panic attacks as adults. Nonetheless, they grow up to be good listeners, accustomed to thinking things through before speaking or taking action. If shyness is due to lack of self-confidence, it can lead to a life spent watching from the sidelines rather than daring to join in.

Emotionally speaking

Men are admired for expressing their feelings; it's important for boys to learn this, and easier when fathers set an example. Besides inheriting characteristics, children learn from modelling and mirroring, the opposite of 'Don't do as I do, do as I say.' Confident people are regarded as cool, but may appear rather controlled, keeping emotions in check.

Feeling funny

Opinions differs as to the number of basic emotions: either four or six – only one of which is good: happiness. At least when we're joyful, it overcomes every other feeling, because it results from the absence of anger, fear and/or sadness (surprise and disgust), the emotions (or combination) from which all others come: envy, shame, and so on. In children, fear usually makes them freeze; adults opt for flight or fight. That adrenalin rush is almost identical to the intense physical reaction to joy: heart pounding, feeling shaky, sometimes energizing us to get up on that stage and show what we're made of. Or we withdraw into ourselves, to try and escape.

Children and emotions

When children are sad, sometimes they want lots of attention and affection, sometimes to be left in peace. Babies let rip with joyful chuckles or bellow with hunger or weariness, but toddlers are overwhelmed by strong emotions and need to learn skills to cope. Lack of emotional competence ('I just lost control') leads to phenomena like road rage. How we deal with emotions is based on what we learned as youngsters. When angry, children hit out and need to learn to moderate their feelings, let go by saying what they feel, without harming others. They may need help acquiring the right vocabulary, but can also draw or play games, working on a scale of one to ten. They also become confused about their emotions because of their parents' reaction. If the latter don't have a clue how to deal with feelings, they round on youngsters: 'Don't make a fuss.' Children then believe that negative emotions mean they're horrible or doing harm, and disappointing their parents. Learning to handle emotion on the outside, means they can deal with what they feel inside.

Most of us imagine we have a natural talent for communication and empathy; parents think they 'know best' and that they 'understand'.

But our emotions make us as likely to get upset with other people by assuming that's their aim, as we do when they're deliberately hurtful. All adult relationships, in every area, depend upon managing emotions, but there aren't that many frank and open discussions, or satisfactory outcomes. How often do we agree to differ, avoiding the issue rather than seeking resolution? Or relegate it to a subtext, telling somebody off for not doing something, rather than revealing what we feel: that it's proof they don't care about us? Depending on the circumstances, action may need to be postponed, but take it out on the pillow, giving it a good thumping when you make the bed.

Feeling down

There is a positive side to negative emotions: anger ensures self-preservation, fear means security, whilst sadness is a cleansing process; it eases away pain so we can move on and rejoin the world. There are umpteen reasons for parents to get upset, but if they simply announce 'I'm angry', children can also get into the habit, and they should be encouraged to explain, and say what they need, rather than what's enraged them. Fears can often be allayed by refusing to allow them room to grow, whilst planning makes life much easier; involving children soothes their worries. Pay attention to what bothers them, then they can learn to speak up for themselves and try new things. Don't discourage him from sobbing (yes, him). Men are notoriously awkward about crying so tell them tears contain chemicals which act as a type of anaesthetic.

Attention!

Parents react more strongly to certain emotions, and children soon learn to take advantage, to get attention or to get their own way: anger turns into tantrums; sadness leads to sulking; fear results in shyness. What could be worse than going on your own somewhere new where nobody knows you, or more humiliating than everybody in the whole room looking at you, and talking about you and laughing at you? Truth is, most people won't notice you, and if they do, they're only mildly curious. Children more easily adapt to new things when parents are practical; for toddlers at the 'scary strangers' stage, make it easier when newcomers visit by sticking to simple introductions.

Mark's dad calls him in to say hello to Mrs Bissett, encouraging him to make eye contact, then sends him back to play with his toys. His mum's pleased: 'Thought you were going to talk him into doing his latest party trick.' Mark has a knack for an uncannily side-splitting version of the latest band's number one, but he'll soon show it off without any encouragement from his parents.

Sulking is a form of emotional blackmail and children should swiftly learn such tactics are pointless. Well, you know what they say about blackmail? Trying to win round a sulky child is a waste of time, teaching them they're going about things exactly the right way. If they choose to punish themselves by cutting off their nose, don't show sympathy. Try agreeing with them; surprise can make them snap out of it. Sulky parents are worse, punishing a child with days of silence or an atmosphere you could cut with a knife, accompanied by a 'dog-faced' look, that blank expression shutting out the other person. Negating a child's existence will convince them that they are totally worthless.

When we believe our feelings are unacceptable, personally or as far as society is concerned, repressing them leads to greater repression, even depression, cancer or heart disease. The more we bottle things up, the greater the risk of explosion, which just goes to prove we were right to mistrust our animal instincts. Feelings become twisted, natural warmth is disguised as coldness, and if we feel our terrible feelings mean we're terrible people, then that's how we behave.

Emotionally prepared

There are ways of expressing our feelings to enhance communication and understanding, and we can contain them so that they're present, neither repressed nor expressed. We should aim to be direct, but fear making a fool of ourselves because it takes practice, experience and wisdom to be effective. It requires balance: aware when to hold back or not, without harming others or putting them on their guard. Anger alone can arise from fear or hatred, used to hurt others, to defend ourselves or protect those we love; we may need to explode to get through: fight fire with fire and turn the tables, though it shouldn't be routine behaviour to solve problems.

Avoiding blame includes self-blame. Nobody is indispensable, so ascertain exactly what your role is and that of other people. Aim to bridge any gaps, e.g. if somebody is jealous, they keep it quiet because that's a bad thing to be, but continue to be resentful. In fact, to the other person, it could be perceived as a compliment. People with little confidence are apt to be somewhat paranoid; when somebody is ignoring you, it's usually because they're furiously busy, not because they're furious with you or don't like you. Yet another vicious circle: the more you're suspicious of others, the more they are wary of you, and the more suspicious you become. It's too true: just because you're paranoid doesn't mean they aren't after you.

Put things into perspective by always trying to assume the best. Or else talk to somebody about it, or ask the person concerned outright. You may opt for a more spiritual solution, whether your beliefs centre on God or a Being, a life-force, being good, etc. People either never mention this or proselytize, but generally, we are now more accepting of Eastern practices, like acupuncture, and the old ways, crystals, etc. Being at peace aids clearer thinking; find your own place, perhaps somewhere outdoors when you're walking, or a favourite view from your window. To maintain balance, we may also need to change: habits, diet, friends, situation, career, aims. Practise self-management, easing the pressure and arranging your life to allow for your own needs. Just as each week has the weekend, have something to look forward to every day.

Arguing the toss – and about every other little thing that comes along

Some people claim to enjoy arguments, being the sign of a healthy relationship. Besides, if children haven't learned to deal with conflict, how will they fare in the world outside? Families which insist that nobody ever argues in their house deny children to chance to experiment, or even to question things, but though most argue sometimes, many seem always to be rowing. It can clear the air, but constant falling out affects children's confidence when it boils down to who's right (parent) and who's wrong (child). It's more important to solve problems by working together, learning to negotiate and to compromise. And children shouldn't have to repress anything negative, pretending everything is hunky dory.

Hot spots

As a parent, what makes you angry? Trick question. Emotions are triggered by something, but your reaction is up to you. It's tricky to come to grips with; when livid, we resent advice about letting it be like 'water off a duck's back'. Quick questionnaire: you've bought somebody a gift, but they're obviously none too thrilled. Are you:

1 Furious. You spent a hell of a lot of time and money.
2 Guilty. Pretty certain it wasn't what they wanted anyway.
3 Resentful – or indifferent. You don't much like them, but felt obliged.
4 Sorry for them, or even amused. They wouldn't be pleased if it were the moon on a stick, and that's always been their attitude, as you well know.

Face up to your own contribution. Parents with low self-esteem, fatally, think along these lines: 'If my children loved me, they'd never do such things/they'd do as they're told.' Mix in some guilt: 'If I can't get them to be tidy/considerate, that proves I'm not a good parent.' But keep it in perspective; if somebody 'makes' you upset or angry, you're saying that their opinion of you matters more than your own. In effect, allowing them power over you.

Children's quick quiz. Your dad's complaining about the bathroom, strewn with damp and dirty towels yet again. He reckons that lack of consideration and messiness would drive anybody crazy. What next?

1 He leaves the bathroom as it is, ignoring complaints that's there's

nothing worse than having a shower then realizing there's no dry towels.

2 He secretly hopes you'll pick everything up and stick it in the washing machine (he never had to sit an exam to work any domestic appliance, not even the video).

3 He refuses to wash any towels for a week.

4 He wakes you up by dumping the towels on top of the bed; maybe not quite what's meant by getting in touch with your inner child.

Things always develop along the same old lines: 'I was in a mad rush!' (instant response: 'Get ready earlier') or 'It's no big deal!' (simple answer: 'Then YOU deal with it'). How do children learn it's OK leave the place in a mess? Because parents automatically cleaned it up. It's not easy to sort out situations once they're well established. You don't want a mess in your nice, clean bathroom and you don't want to fall out with your nice, clean children. Discussion and decision are the answer, once you decide to stick to what you say.

Rows make us revel in self-pity or resort to emotional blackmail; anger and resentment result in people doing something 'just to prove it', to spite others (revenge) or themselves (martyrdom). Habitual arguing encourages a lack of self-discipline, yet fosters the need to control, and gives people the opportunity to avoid responsibility. It's easier to keep arguing than deal with the upheaval change brings about. The knock-on effect means it spills over into other areas, taking it out on others when unable to confront the people responsible. But is it 'them'? Could it be you?

Getting to the bottom of it all

Whatever sparks it off, arguments rapidly fire up into each side trying to convince the other to see their point of view. If you get lost on holiday, is the one reading the map to blame, or the other for being too impatient to follow directions? Better to stop wasting time and find out where you are.

We're accustomed to referring to 'sub-text' in conversation, but there are three layers in all:

• First: what's all this about?

• Second: what's it really about, i.e. your true feelings, and how arguing subsequently affects them.

• Finally, and most important: the impact on your very self: your identity.

Your assumptions, plus the other person's, affect your self-image. They make you question everything you stand for and how others see you, and drive big holes in your self-esteem.

Communication breakdown

How often do we say 'I didn't mean what I said'? More trouble is caused because we don't say what we mean, or can't say it. When it's hard to express our emotions or share our feelings, a communication breakdown signals failure, which affects self-confidence. Proceed slowly. What do you really mean? What do you really think? What do you really think about me, and vice versa?

Feelings are so strong they need to be discussed, yet that depth makes it seem impossible to articulate them. Learning understanding and empathy helps us all, as does diplomacy; we pride ourselves on our ability to communicate, rather than paying attention properly. Misunderstandings are common; somebody who practises reflective listening, i.e. repeating the other person's words to show they're following what was said, could have their consideration misconstrued as mockery. Providing it's discussed at the time, rather than one going off brooding and the other entirely unaware, it can be solved.

To an outsider, it's often clear what's gone wrong, and that both sides actually make sense. But being insistent on our need to be understood, we don't heed the other's version, or even want to. Naturally it differs from our own, which is based on our view of life: what we see, what we know, what we feel. With each aspect being interpreted individually, it's bound to diverge. Being keener to express ourselves rather than heed what's being said, we fail to appreciate that understanding the other point of view doesn't necessarily mean giving in, or even agreeing. We should be curious about their side of the story – hard at first to feign, but expressing it, even a little, suggests an attempt to meet halfway, encouraging reciprocation. It also shows respect. When this is mutual, it does wonders for everybody's confidence.

Red for go

By recognizing the danger signs (i.e. body language) in others, and ourselves, we can attempt to avoid conflict:

- Change of tone of voice and breathing; pupils dilating and face turning red; making fists or threatening gestures.
- Step back; gain a breathing space: ask questions/advice, find out more from others.
- Don't become abusive or make accusations.
- Show you're paying attention; adopt reflective listening.
- Concentrate on finding a solution rather than sticking up for your rights: what do you want and what do they want; how to bring it about; or agree to differ.

Help yourself keep calm, bring anger down to annoyance:

- Need for justification/retaliation.
- In fact, do you really need all this? Why do you feel like this?
- Balance your resistance and their point of view.
- Circumstances (yours and theirs); other things make matters worse, and is this going to lead to more trouble for you from others, e.g. family?

When we're stressed, we have less patience; anger makes us seek either a safety valve or a whipping boy. But more confidence, less stress, equals fewer problems.

Part 3 Low life: problems associated with lack of confidence, and some solutions

Risky business

Not adolescents again? Well, no, because these problems can manifest even earlier: girls pregnant at ten; primary school children committing crimes. All parents should be aware that all children could end up in trouble; this section contains scenarios involving youngsters with ample confidence. Similarly, gender is a factor; consumption of drink and drugs is greater in all-male groups than those of mixed sex, though this seems to be increasingly the case with gangs of girls, notoriously when on holiday. Many tour companies ban the hire of accommodation to single-sex parties.

What are the odds?

Some of us take risks, others don't, but a few do their damndest to take it to the limit. So many teenagers have a bone-deep conviction in their invincibility: 'It'll never happen to me', as much a puzzle to parents as their suddenly skin-deep vulnerability, and they often belong to a gang, whether leader of the pack or hanging on, to avoid being an outcast. Confident children know they can't lose (leading a charmed life). Those with low self-esteem have nothing to lose (at its worst, this could be equated with a death wish).

Youngsters who have the most problems are more inclined to commit crimes as individuals; often pre-planned, their intent is more serious. Gang members experiment or act on impulse, egging each other on as a dare or for a laugh.

Keeping on the straight and narrow

Two things which should help your children – not chains and padlocks on their bedroom doors, but supervision and discipline. Setting clear limits helps prevent aggression and anti-social behaviour; whatever punishment is meted out should involve some form of recompense, like cleaning up graffiti. Inconsistent discipline is unsettling, e.g. sudden loss of temper, or constant changes of mind, when instructions are insufficiently comprehensible, especially since children are blamed for not carrying them out properly. Likewise, when parents cannot agree or support each other, ending up with the old 'good cop, bad cop' routine. The more heavy-handed one parent tends to be (mother or father), the more the other challenges the rule by rushing to protect the poor little thing, or subverts it, by encouraging the child to be deceitful. Matters are complicated when each clearly has a favourite.

Parents who are forever rowing often don't give children sufficient affection or exercise control. If they are over-indulgent or neglectful, lack of discipline gives children too much responsibility, and when this happens from an early age, they've no idea how to handle it. They feel inadequate, as they do when parents are authoritarian or over-protective, depriving them of autonomy. Habitually yelling at your children, or hitting them, teaches them that's how to respond. Tell them repeatedly they're bad, and they behave badly. Children want to feel secure; if their needs aren't met, they become frustrated. If they have to look after one or other parent (even both) because the latter can't cope with problems (violence, debts, etc,), it can encourage aggressive behaviour.

Future forecast

To end on a more positive note, there are some signs of success with certain issues, e.g. using seat belts and drink driving. With smoking, though it's reported that more young girls have taken it up, cigarettes are increasingly being stamped out; one day, it will be something you'll be able to do only in the comfort of your own home (or out on the back porch). However, prohibition could put tobacco on a par with illegal drugs, glamorizing it in teenagers' eyes; it's also been suggested that people may turn to drugs and/or alcohol instead of cigarettes. As for AIDS and HIV, it may once have seemed that investing in rubber guaranteed early retirement as a millionaire; back in 1986–87, condom sales rose by 20 per cent, but haven't continued to increase at that rate. 'In moderation' is the key phrase and parents can console themselves that extreme cases are in the minority.

The last few years of the twentieth century saw a huge surge of interest in health. New Age practices are so popular, few would associate them with what might, in the not-too-distant past, have been castigated as the casting of spells, whether white or black magic. Many people now know a great deal about health matters, for example the causes of stress (the effect such things as crime or gambling have on families as a whole) and the illnesses caused by stress. However, it's still difficult to prevent problems leading to drink and drugs, sexual promiscuity and eating disorders, not to mention curing them. Nevertheless, with parents being more aware, they can help their children be more confident, thus avoiding or solving most problems.

Peer pressure

Something of a conundrum: belonging to certain groups requires you to be non-conformist, i.e. against the Establishment, yet obliges you to conform to the group itself. Confident people are prepared to take risks, and won't always follow the crowd. Those with low self-esteem sometimes don't see themselves as having an existence apart from other people.

Under the influence

Opinion is divided on the influence of peer pressure, and though it's usually associated with teenagers, the under-tens are believed to be more susceptible; even groups of young children gang up to outwit their teacher. Traditionally (reassuringly), though, experts claim that youngsters who have a good relationship with their parents are less influenced, particularly when taught to trust their instincts and learn empathy, so that they care about other people and value friendship.

Now, however, never mind nature/nurture, and parents in particular, peer pressure is said to be largely responsible for the way people turn out. Parenting has changed dramatically in recent years, e.g. smacking being frowned upon, but children's behaviour is not radically different. It's even felt they may learn from other parents as much as their own, i.e. the families of their peers. And what of sibling pressure? Whether brothers and sisters are close or not, when moving in the same circles, children tend to follow their elders' lead, particularly where smoking, alcohol and drugs are involved, and the last two frequently have links with crime.

It cannot be denied that the last thing any self-respecting teenager wants is to have anything whatsoever in common with grown-ups in general, his parents in particular. Youngsters inhabit a world of their own; it's what's going on there and the other members who matter. However, the degree to which they are affected by peer pressure is down to self-esteem, though the phrase itself is perhaps a misnomer. 'Peer' implies all children are equal, which is hardly accurate, nor do they all spend all their time actively coaxing or bullying others into doing something. It's more subtle than that, even insidious. Teenagers need to feel they belong, as we all do, to establish their own identity, and identify with other people. The pressure activating our behaviour or attitude comes from what we feel inside, addressing our own needs. No matter what the circumstances, it is always our decision, even though we may feel pressurized into making it. We have a choice.

Carl's teacher hands out cards showing a set of parallel lines, the outer two being clearly longer. Half the group have been primed to say they're the same length, and so do the rest, even when clearly perplexed, rather than go against general opinion. Not Carl, and he's pleased that he's the only one to disagree.

Everybody's doing it

Good children may be curious about the way others behave, or about their attitude, and even experiment; they're usually more tolerant than their parents. But they rarely do bad things by accident, or solely because of others. Is it attitude which determines what group you belong to, or is it the group which determines your attitude? Packs of baddies act even worse, through lack of social controls. Nice children stick together, although decent individuals still get swept up; easier to lose control when everyone around has, hence mob rule. In sport (other than team games), peer pressure can give rise to cheating and aggression – with greater effect on girls.

The peer group provides teenagers with support and encouragement, easing separation anxiety so that they can be apart from their parents, gain independence and face the adult world. Along with gang rules and family rules, young people also have to learn to conform, and acquire the necessary social skills. Sometimes, the wrong crowd seems to transform a Goody Two-Shoes overnight into the big bad wolf; parents blame peer pressure for leading children astray, yet they usually underestimate its power. Children may be less conscious of this. They've grown up with peer pressure, and being deeply embedded makes it more powerful. It's a process of evolving; the more time they spend outside the home, the more they adapt to the different culture.

Besides, parents are also influenced by peer pressure. Few can withstand the demands of fashion; their children have to have what everybody else is wearing; youngsters have been mugged when wearing the latest trainers, and bullied for wearing the wrong clothes. Nor would most adults wear a suit to a football match or Bermudas to a posh wedding. They also have to deal with peer pressure at work and amongst their friends; different spheres of influence have certain views and behaviour in common: what WOULD the neighbours say?

Teenage outrage

Although adolescents are renowned for being rebels, with or without a cause, they demonstrate their individuality by being virtually identical to the rest of their crowd. Uniformity, e.g. jeans and T-shirts, makes a fashion statement. Most of us do conform, one way or another, because we need to belong to a group or to a community. People who choose to go their own way, even when part of the crowd, may be considered cool, but they're often regarded as eccentric, even looked at with suspicion. You need healthy self-esteem to do this, though it's a pleasure to really be yourself, able to wear, and to do, what suits you. It also takes as much confidence to go against general opinion, no matter what the topic, or to stick up for your friends.

Tarring birds of a feather

The underclass, largely made up of young men, is seen as the biggest threat to society; it's largely regarded as 'normal' for teenagers to be delinquent, due to factors like poverty, environment and unemployment. Pundits also blame families. Lack of a father figure is believed to result in an all too familiar attitude: aggressive, macho, uncommunicative, wouldn't know a sense of humour if it hit them on the funny bone. At worst, it includes every 'ism' and phobia going. The peer group becomes family.

When parents take little interest in their children, they are unlikely to have other role models or mentors: relatives, teachers or employers. Figures of authority earn nothing but contempt; even in the average family, if adolescents automatically challenge their parents, they will oppose authority. Boys who lack role models are more likely to get involved in crime, and their aggression is exacerbated by various factors, like being the first generation in centuries when there's no major war. Joining gangs could be said to be a primitive impulse, running with the pack. With some children, it's a kind of pressure valve; they feel they can truly be themselves or else explore their own potential, revealing hitherto unknown traits. If parents cannot make their children's friends feel at home, whilst keeping a eye on the situation and encouraging them to take up other group activities, they should avoid dictating who those friends should be.

Until the early 1970s, most young men automatically went from school to a job, but gradually, fewer openings became available with the increasing number of women going to work. Nowadays, many boys regret not making the most of their education, but claim that schools don't encourage them to plan for the future, or ease the transition into the workplace, although being stuck in jobs they hate is often what makes them go to college. The macho culture prevents them for asking for help from any source, from newspapers to job centre, or taking advice; they heed only their siblings and their peers in a similar situation.

In the good old days, boys were apprenticed, or had a job to go to, mainly following in Dad's footsteps. It provided security, continuity, responsibility, and a wage, and working so hard and for such long hours, they didn't have the energy, or the opportunity, to get into trouble. We wouldn't wish such a hard time on our children, but when they're unable to get a job, encourage them to get involved in something, such as voluntary work, not because 'the devil finds work for idle hands' but because helping others makes people feel worthwhile and responsible.

Aiming for As

The following helps children to stay confident and resist peer pressure:

- Analysing (relationships; situations; positives; negatives).
- Assessing (monitoring; improvements).
- Acknowledging (nobody and nothing can be perfect).
- Awareness (all five senses; spirituality).
- Attitude (positive, not negative).
- Action: only a few minutes are needed each day to practise what you've learned.

Eating disorders I: slim pickings

Each year, anorexia results in one or two fatalities (see pp. 71–3), plus related deaths (suicide, heart failure, etc.) and for many parents nowadays, it ranks alongside drugs as their worst nightmare; the newsletter for the National Centre for Eating Disorders has a readership of 3,000, but many more sufferers do not acknowledge the problem. Disorders also include obesity, compulsive eating (bingeing and dieting), and bulimia (bingeing and vomiting), and low self-esteem is said to be the main cause. When sufferers cannot deal with such psychological problems, they are thought to be getting rid of them, either through vomiting or actual weight loss. Problems can also be forgotten or ignored, because eating disorders take up so much time and energy.

Appetite for destruction

With bulimia and compulsive eating, when weight remains stable and there are few obvious signs (continual vomiting can result in a puffy face), they may consequently be as dangerous as anorexia and obesity. Many people feel sick at the idea of deliberately making themselves throw up, and it ultimately results in tooth decay, dehydration, etc.; bulimics also use laxatives, which get rid of water, not weight. Parents should watch out for medicines which can have similar side-effects. Anorexics sometimes binge, hardly surprising when they're starving, but tend to pride themselves on being in control, whilst bulimics hate their uncontrollable needs. Neither ever feels satisfied.

Almost anyone on a diet could be termed a compulsive eater because food is all they think about. The main reason people give up is because they give in and go on a binge, although in the long run, it's more effective exercising regularly and eating less, and sensibly. Occasional treats do little harm; there's no point in starving, or giving up completely, to carry on stuffing yourself. Or going back on yet another diet, though nearly every female could tell you, right this minute, exactly what she weighs. Getting on the scales to discover you've lost weight gives you a tremendous buzz. That incredible feeling, the sense of achievement, explains how easy it is to become obsessed, especially for people who rarely feel good about anything they do.

Soul food

From childhood, eating is a source of comfort, and more so while growing up and facing all kinds of stress. Furthermore, society equates slenderness with success; in parts of the world where being thin isn't a priority, there are few cases of eating disorders. Historically, an ample figure was valued as a sign of prosperity, whilst fasting was associated with religious and spiritual beliefs. Saintly people believed it was good for the soul, bringing them closer to their gods (it probably did; lack of food can give you a high). People still go on hunger strike for a cause, and they're seen as heroic. Fashion-wise, fasting is recommended for more earthly reasons, to improve your health. There's even a recent notion that it's possible to live on fresh air. The association with self-sacrifice suggests that denying yourself food makes you a better person. What puzzles most people is those who keep stuffing themselves with colossal amounts of food, even raw or frozen, not even enjoying what they're eating.

Fat-free?

With today's growing emphasis on health and beauty, few people appear to be satisfied with either appetite or appearance. Constantly informed that 'you cannot be too rich or too thin', whilst the number of obese people (including children) is steadily increasing (along with accusations of 'fatism'), many of us end up confused. Food, any and many kinds of it, has never been so widely available, and neither have all the warnings about it. Not to mention dieting.

In America, about two-thirds of the population are on a diet at any one time. In this country, about one-third of women are over-weight and nearly half the men; it's said to add over six years to your age. But the gap narrows with obesity: around one-fifth of women, slightly fewer men. Anyone who comes up with a sure-fire way to lose weight *and keep it off* would end up a trillionaire. If they could solve the problem of anorexia, they'd deserve every penny. With the number of cases growing in the past 20 years, the media seems to have been a powerful influence. Those in the public eye, in demanding careers like sport or modelling, are known for a high incidence of eating disorders; one sizeable celebrity did slim down from around a size 20 to wear a size 12 wedding dress.

Some people believe anorexia in young women results from the desire to avoid growing up. Rather than attempt to make the most of themselves, they think they should make themselves something different, to fit in with the demands of society. Since the onset of puberty can be from seven to 14, with so many changes, including shape, dieting is generally pointless until it's over. Puppy fat does go away, but some parents go on about children keeping an eye on their weight. Sometimes, that's been the mother's principal occupation:

crash diets, wonder diets, latest fashion diets.

Weighty problems

Teenagers are prone to bad hair days, and every variation. It's thought that moaning about 'being fat' covers a multitude of sins, i.e. whatever they're secretly most worried about. But we all have deep, dark fears, never realizing that (a) they're really not that terrible; and (b) plenty of others have the same troubles.

> Janie is generally very confident, but when she asks her mum about her new dress, the latter isn't concentrating and forgets that the correct (immediate) response is 'You look nice.' She hesitates, then murmurs that Janie will give herself back problems if she doesn't stand up straight. What about the dress? 'Perhaps it's a wee bit clingy?' Next thing, Janie's ringing round her friends, proclaiming: 'Mum says I look fat.'

It's no good protesting that you never said anything of the kind, children couldn't be more offended if you told them their bum does look big in that. No matter how confident you are, sometimes some things really do get to you.

Eating disorders II: anorexia

Now regarded as a disease, if anorexia results in the body denied essential nutrients, which eventually affects the brain, it could account for the rigid behaviour of sufferers. Unable to regulate their appetite, there comes a point when they feel as sick with not eating as when they eat. They also suffer from sleeplessness, weariness, dizziness, severe constipation, bad circulation (causing constant fidgeting), poor hair condition. In extreme cases, anorexics are hospitalized, having to undergo unpleasant treatment because of the damage to their body: absence of periods, kidney damage, and so on. Emphasis is on the need to get them eating again, but reward systems or withdrawal of privileges may prove short-term solutions. It's now thought better to discover why they had recourse to something so drastic, e.g. some form of therapy and/or self-help groups; besides low self-esteem, anorexics are frequently perfectionists, and/or victims of neglect or abuse. Wasting away, wasting their lives, they need someone who listens to them.

Some youngsters envy this willpower, wishing they could as easily resist eating fattening foods. Wrong way round; anorexics need as much self-control to make themselves eat something. One of the first effects of stress is to act as an appetite depressant, as much when we fall in love as when we're going through a rough patch. A bar of chocolate usually cheers us up, but we can rarely face breakfast on the morning of an exam.

In control; out of control

People who feel worthless and vile on the inside seem to need make this clear to the outside world; people know what an advanced case of anorexia looks like from those which hit the headlines. But anorexics can't see a near skeleton in the mirror, just somebody who desperately needs to lose weight. The desire to slim often triggers it off, even in people who barely have a pick on them. Maybe they think the boy they fancy will then fancy them, or their boyfriend would prefer them slimmer? Maybe a friend makes a comment or joke (or was being ironic)? Maybe everything will be fine, once they reach their ideal weight? By then, depriving themselves of food is a habit.

Power corrupts; absolute power corrupts absolutely. Anorexia gives its victims immense power. It puts them in total control, maybe for the first time in their lives, paradoxically, by being incapable of controlling the refusal to eat. High achievers demonstrate their need to control as the kind of good children who aim to live up to their parents' expectations as well as their own (if not more so), never known to rebel against anything. But when they believe they're loved for what they've done, and not for what they are, any mistake or failure means they completely let their parents down.

Anorexics are usually girls, though boys are also affected, as well as older women. They end up insatiably driven to deny themselves nourishment. Sometimes they're regarded as selfish, punishing those closest to them; parents cannot ignore a child constantly threatened with death. This kind of living suicide could be described as the ultimate emotional blackmail.

Slender chances

Since we all have a different metabolism, what we consume has varying effects on our bodies. We also have different kinds of mind-set, some more addictive than others, and if anorexics weren't focused on food, it could have been alcohol, drugs or gambling. However, sometimes it may be possible to direct that drive for control towards something purposeful, even hobbies and activities, though parents are warned about sport; anorexics tend to be compulsive about exercise.

Love and food provide vital nourishment; women are praised for home cooking, the way to a man's heart. Refusing food because you're hurt, angry or sad, is a way of spurning love. Eating disorders are more easily solved in the early stages, so where families eat together, a child with erratic eating habits may be more noticeable, although when mealtimes are the setting for rows, it distracts from such behaviour. It also exacerbates it, then parents complain about children disobeying them by not eating properly, food being wasted, time and effort spent preparing meals. In fact, many anorexics prepare elaborate meals for the rest of the household, without touching a morsel, although with time being at a premium, work or leisure, 'grazing' is common, with snacks taken when required, especially with young people. This, plus the fashion for baggy clothing, aids and abets teenagers with eating disorders; they become inordinately secretive, concealing the problem until it's full-blown.

Food for thought: suggestions and solutions

Allowing for phases, if you have any suspicions, don't assume this problem will fade away. Dispense with the scales; anyone needing to keep on eye on their weight can arrange an appointment at the doctor's or nearest clinic. What's your children's attitude towards food? They all have fads, invariably going off something the minute you purchase the giant economy size. But do they fuss about eating in public? Do they classify food as 'good' or 'bad'? Compulsive eaters and bulimics feel too much guilt to enjoy eating, anorexics too much fear.

Toddlers want to eat when they're hungry, but are expected to fit in with family mealtimes. Parents should be relaxed, and avoid forcing them to eat, allowing for different tastes. There's no reason why children can't go shopping for what they want to eat, or learn about nutrition. Encourage them to take an interest in planning their own meals, then cooking for themselves, especially if they're fussy eaters. Highly sensitive children can detect tiny variations in flavour, and feel hunger strongly, needing to eat to avoid a drop in energy levels.

There are no miracle cures. Progress is slow because it's so hard for anorexics to learn how to eat normally again. They rarely feel comfortable eating with others, or dealing with comments, even praise. Once weight gain shows improved health, such as periods starting again, it's a good time to tackle underlying problems. Parents should encourage children to be realistic and positive, able to ask for help and support. Remind them when they feel awful about putting weight back on, it's still not as bad as being anorexic. If they do binge, rather than react by depriving themselves again, they should understand no harm is done if they simply go back to eating normally.

Stress I: depression and anxiety

Recent forecasts indicate that depression, now classed as an illness, will soon be the second most common illness. Anxiety can be just as unbearable. This, like long-term stress, may lead to depression, and people can suffer from both at the same time. Those with little confidence are prone to stress because molehills immediately assume mountainous proportions, whilst the first thing to hit people suffering from anxiety and/or depression is loss of confidence. In fact, too little stress is bad for you, making life boring and stagnant, but a small amount can help you get things done.

When everything gets you down

We know life ain't fair, but not everybody is equipped to deal with that, and while sensitive people may be enviably gifted, it's at the cost of painfully thin skin. They react to stimuli far more intensely than the average person, who, when they miss a bus, assume there'll be another along in a minute.

> Dean is highly sensitive, and highly likely to imagine the worst: missing the bus sets up a chain reaction. The next bus will be held up (if it turns up), making him late for work, so he'll be barred from that vital conference. Then he'll lose his job. Then he'll go bankrupt and lose all his possessions, totally disowned by friends and family.

This is not to mock, but to put things into perspective. Whenever parent or child is unaccountably late, the person waiting soon puts two and two together and becomes 100 per cent convinced of disaster. Imagination is a wonderful thing, but can be a curse. To improve empathy with somebody who is highly sensitive, remember that when it is sparked off by something you think exceptionally trivial, the depth of their emotion should be compared with what most scares or angers you. Many adults who are prone to stress believe the answer lies in their early years, and a troubled childhood has a greater impact on those who are highly sensitive. However, a healthy childhood seems to help prevent them from suffering unduly from stress.

The two imposters

Anxiety is the old fight or flight reflex – in full flight. Depression is failure to respond, 'playing dead'. Two sides of the same coin, they have certain elements in common, physical and mental: headaches and aches and pains; fatigue; insomnia; loss of appetite; inability to concentrate; fear of sickness.

There are also distinct differences. With anxiety you blame outside causes: get tense and agitated; thoughts speed up; performance at anything deteriorates (obsessing about it); worsens towards evenings. And when depressed, you blame yourself: slump and become lethargic; thoughts slow down; performance at anything deteriorates (indifference); worse in the morning.

People who succumb to stress may be dismissed as neurotic: invariably depressed or attacked by anxiety; unhealthy attitude towards relationships, either clingy or avoidant. Depression and anxiety may not be long term (though it's impossible to believe it at the time) but in reaction to circumstances, major upheavals such as births, marriages, divorce and deaths. Teenagers are known for turbulent emotions, and it's now recognized that pre-teens also suffer from stress, even children as young as four.

Depression

Said to affect over one in 20 of 14- to 16-year-olds, depression is thought to result from a flaw in the brain's neurotransmitters (e.g. serotonin), i.e. brain cells failing to communicate properly, perhaps due to long-term stress. The result is overwhelming negativity. Sufferers feel worthless and helpless, filled with guilt, brooding over mistakes and failures, distanced from their nearest and dearest. Trapped by a total inability to motivate yourself to do anything, it's like being held prisoner in a room where the door is ajar. Nobody would wish it on their worst enemy. People spend most of their time sleeping, or they're plagued by insomnia and lying in bed makes it ten times worse, unable to escape from all those black thoughts. Sometimes brought on by external events, depression could be deemed a natural reaction, but when there appears to be no apparent reason, that in itself makes the sufferer feel worse.

Making it easier on yourself

At crisis point, anti-depressants can help; they may take two to three weeks to work but enable people to carry on, preventing them from descending to the depths. However, while reducing tension and repressing anxiety, they affect sensitivity and some people feel like they're on auto-pilot. Physical symptoms can be solved by medication: headaches and stomachaches; sleeplessness and exhaustion; trembling; sweating; blushing; heart pounding; sick stomach; muscle tension; inability to concentrate, i.e. difficulty in listening and communicating; forgetfulness; being accident prone. Left unchecked, such symptoms lead to poor health, weight gain or loss, high blood-pressure, and ultimately ulcers, heart disorders and cancer. Watch out for danger signs, especially when facing tricky situations; when pressure is piling on, it's time to ease off: irritability; loss of appetite; indecisive; unable to concentrate; problems sleeping; muscle tension (shoulders aiming to join up with your ear lobes is a giveaway).

Try a more strategic approach, even a total revamp of lifestyle, starting by eating well and reading up on nutrition. Take up exercise. not just sport, but yoga, meditation and relaxation. Try aromatherapy or massage; inner peace encourages a sense of enormous well-being, as Blur assure us in 'Park Life'. Adopt skills which help you retain a sense of humour and be more philosophical, keeping everything in perspective. Be organized (making lists etc.), tidy, more assertive. Learn to cope with change by asking others for help or preparing yourself, finding out everything you need to know. What about self-help? Talking to somebody and/or writing everything down gets things out of your system. A diary is useful, being cathartic, but an analytical approach may be better, e.g. some kind of chart to monitor situations.

Investigate psychology, etc, but don't overdo it; reading about anxiety and depression can bring it on. If you're after something more professional, the discussions are aimed at uncovering past traumas or what's been repressed. This enables you to live fully in the present, rather than forever blanking out your troubles, something workaholics and control freaks are prone to do. Cognitive behavioural techniques teach you to examine irrational beliefs leading to feelings of hopelessness, i.e. the sheer impossibility of statements: why is everybody always so horrible to me? Logically, nobody can be subjected 24 hours a day to non-stop unpleasantness from every single person. You can learn skills to avoid dark thoughts, and alleviate stress. Taking on simple, specific tasks helps bolster confidence: setting realistic goals to learn problem-solving, and rewarding yourself.

Stress II: suicidal tendencies

Few things are more tragic than the death of a child; when they have killed themselves, it is particularly hard for family and friends to deal with.

Suicide is stigmatized in the West; in Japan, where it's regarded as the honourable thing to do, there are 30,000 cases per annum. The UK total is about 4,000 each year, around one in five deaths. Every hour of every day, several people kill themselves; attempts are made nearly every five minutes. In 1997, nearly 800 young people died: two each day. Suicide is one of the ten most common causes of death for students (in Belfast, the rate is about one a month). Nineteen thousand make suicide attempts, young women more than young men (and by less violent means), but the latter usually succeed. The rate is steadily increasing; in 1995: nearly 20 per cent of deaths in the 15–24 age group. For men 25–44, it has doubled in the past 25 years; for under 35s it is higher than that of fatal car accidents.

The only way out

What drives people to kill themselves, especially teenagers? Suicide seems to have a bizarre hold on society (so many examples of heroes and heroines), regarded as dramatically glamorous, an almost glorious self-sacrifice. It's also seen as a realistic escape route, and a way to save face, though liable to be tragically accidental, linked with drink or drugs (even Russian roulette). Who hasn't gone to bed one night thinking 'If I were dead, then they'd be sorry.' When the future is unbearably bleak – nothing to enjoy, no hope, no point in going on – suicide seems the only answer.

One of the great taboos, suicide is difficult to talk about, though discussion is probably the main thing which could prevent it. Such stress results from many causes:

- striving for academic excellence;
- break-up of a relationship;
- physical and mental suffering, e.g. chronic illness;
- sacrifice, to make the world a better place, or their family, if they feel so worthless;
- anger and revenge: punishing those nearest to them; as emotional blackmail, it's often resorted to in front of somebody else.

Joey came from a very large family and caused so much trouble all the time, most of them felt it was a relief when he finally killed himself. He had forgotten to buy his mother a card for her birthday.

When people cannot endure life a moment longer, in destroying themselves they condemn those who love them to a lifetime of misery. Nobody knows for certain whether death brings merciful oblivion, but suppose there is an afterlife? To exist for eternity, knowing family and friends really didn't care, or aware of their pain forever?

Danger signals

Suicide is believed to be more common during spring and autumn, and in cities more than in the country, though both the medical profession and farmers have high suicide rates. With the latter reaching one a week, the government has considered revoking rural shotgun licences. There can also be a pattern, a history of suicide or such impulses in the family. Attempts can go wrong either way: surviving, but severely maimed or brain damaged; people taking an overdose don't realize the effect large quantities of drugs have on the body, e.g. paracetamol damaging the liver. Or what's known as a cry for help which ends in death.

It's commonly believed that people who threaten suicide rarely go ahead, but whether hints or announcements, they should be heeded: half the children who kill themselves talked about it or attempted it in the 24 hours beforehand. Parents should note the following:

- Depression, particularly when appearing to show signs of recovering (until that point, they can't summon up the motivation).
- Feelings of guilt, unworthiness or emptiness.
- Problems with alcohol and/or drugs.
- Circumstances: end of relationships or bereavement, particularly dependent personalities.
- Preparation: tidying up possessions or giving them away; hoarding drugs; making a will.

Suicide is clearly a danger for those in a situation where they're affected by loneliness and isolation, but young people can feel like that even when part of one, big happy family. Some, having taken an overdose, ring the Samaritans because they are scared of dying alone. Suicide is also more likely when there have been previous attempts, in particular, where these were violent: guns; drowning; hanging; corrosive poisons; or premeditated, i.e. the person took steps to avoid preventative action. Most cases suffer from clinical depression, and although well over three-quarters visited a doctor in the previous month, few seem to have mentioned their true reasons.

Survival instincts

The need to survive has the power to keep us going, but death sometimes results when people lose the will to live. It has been claimed that if life were indeed so bad that every part of you yearned to die, you'd simply give up and die. Suicide is also described as the coward's way out, yet it must take every ounce of courage to kill yourself. That degree of determination, used to try and hold on, would eventually help ensure that life became more bearable. When family relationships are so bad it drives somebody to contemplate suicide, is it harder to live, and prove them wrong? People don't long for death as such, but a less painful life, failing to realize that killing themselves can be agonizing. Confidence gives children the resilience to believe they can get through, that life may be hell, but it will get better.

Promiscuity and teenage pregnancy

'If you loved me . . .' is often quoted as the reason young ladies slip down the primrose path; if desperately seeking to be loved, they'll fall for that one. Paradoxically, confident youngsters are vulnerable; they presume they'll always be safe.

Figuring it all out

The average age for initial sexual experience is 14 for girls and 13 for boys, and one in three have intercourse before the age of 16. In the 16 to 24 age group, over one-third of girls and about 15 per cent of boys regret losing their virginity at an early age; the younger they were, the more they regret it. Girls appear to be less inhibited these days, and with their behaviour and attitude becoming more laddish, young men, correspondingly, appear to be becoming even more promiscuous. Fathering a child is proof of masculinity; using a condom is not. Many parents do not like the idea that for young people, along with eating and drinking, sex is another everyday appetite; as one student from the depths of the countryside points out, 'What else is there to do?' But the warning 'lies, damned lies and statistics' applies; whether through reticence, or the opposite, it's difficult to get an accurate picture of anybody's sexual behaviour. A line from a Woody Allen film sums it up: the man claims he and his girlfriend hardly ever have sex, 'about three times a week'; she insists they're always having sex – 'about three times a week'.

With statistics based on the number of teenage conceptions, it doesn't give the full picture. Other factors include: contraception; number of partners; urban and rural differences. And different cultures have different views and solutions: total abstinence; early marriage, etc. For under-15s factors include early onset of periods, as well as those influencing under-16s such as early sexual experience; lack of educational goals; sex education from friends and the media rather than schools.

Sexually transmitted diseases (STDs)

HIV and AIDS result from promiscuity and unprotected sex, especially with drink and drugs. There are increasing cases of STDs, which cause pain, discharge, itching, and lumps, and hepatitis B, more infectious than HIV, may cause liver damage. Teenagers suffer from the second highest level of herpes, but higher rates than other groups of women for gonorrhoea, genital warts and chlamydia. Syphilis isn't common in the UK but can cause heart problems and dementia; if contracted during pregnancy, it may result in stillbirth or congenital infections. With gonorrhoea, most women show no symptoms, unlike men; the reverse is true of trichomoniasi (tiny parasites). Herpes is incurable and chlamydia can go undetected and may cause infertility. Genital warts is the most common STD, the highest rate of infection being in girls aged 16 to 19 and men 20 to 24.

Teenage pregnancy: facts and figures

The Government aimed to reduce teenage pregnancies in the 13–15 age group to about 5 in every 1000 by 2000, but this has now changed to under-18s by 2010. The rate is around 9 in every 1000, but in regions with high levels of unemployment and poverty, it's about six times more common: around 12 per 1000 to 17. The highest rate is up North, in Yorkshire, an average of 10 and a half, the lowest being around 7: mostly the South and West; early in the 90s, the rate in Tunbridge Wells was less than the Government target.

There are more teenage single parents in the UK than anywhere else in Western Europe, due to less use of contraception and poorer sex education than increased sexual activity. In 1992, for the first time in ten years, the number of pregnant under-16s fell to nearly 6,000; conceptions in the 15–19 age group fell slightly between 1996 and 1997. Whether girls choose to have the baby or an abortion is fairly evenly split; the latter appears to be the middle-class option.

Sexual healing?

Single-parent teenagers often hit the headlines, although they account for less than 3 per cent, and the majority stay at home; fewer than 10 per cent live with a partner. Conversely, more women are opting for later pregnancies. Parents expect their married offspring to provide grandchildren after a decent interval, but many would agree that marriage or relationships needn't be on the agenda immediately after adolescence. So why is it, with sex, seemingly, all around us, there are so many unplanned pregnancies? The main reasons appear to be ignorance and mixed messages (everybody's doing it, but it's not legal until you're 16, so contraception must be illegal); low expectations; poor prospects; poverty. There are two other main factors: being the child of a teenage mother and girls with emotional difficulties. According to one teacher, you can tell the ones liable to get caught: those who want to work in a nursery or for a vet. It seems inevitable that girls with low self-esteem want something of their own to love.

There's a lot of controversy about sex education. Should it be more widespread, available at an earlier age, or does it lead to greater promiscuity? Back in 1995, where schools were the main source, those girls were least likely to become sexually active before they were 16. And what if access to contraception were easier, in particular the erroneously named 'morning after' pill? With prescriptions tripling, it's largely thought this will be the main factor in reducing the number of under-age conceptions.

Myths and near misses

There are still some strange tales abounding about sex. More than a quarter of girls say they didn't know about contraceptives, or where to get them. It has been calculated that about one-third don't bother, believing the GP would tell their parents. Reasons for not using contraception are wide-ranging, usually because of having sex unexpectedly, and use of the pill is on the decline, largely because of health scares. Girls are reluctant to risk being thought of as slags, or too embarrassed, or assume boys won't bother with condoms. However, most boys reckon they would take precautions, if the girl wanted. As to reasons why teenagers have sex the first time, you'll be delighted to know that it must be love, so well over half reckon. Curiosity is right up there too, at about a third. Being drunk accounts for about 10 per cent, as does peer pressure, and that's twice as much with boys. Pressure from boyfriends is the reason in well over three-quarters of cases.

Confidentiality is a problem; most under-16s, and half the 16- to 19-year-olds, think GPs are bound to tell their parents. Well over three-quarters of 13- to 15-year-olds would discuss contraception with their teacher, unless they felt it would be passed on to their parents. Most teenage girls find out from magazine problem pages, which causes a furore in the daily papers. Many suggestions cause controversy: electronic baby dolls in schools; advertising campaigns in clubs; free supplies of emergency contraception.

Clearly, where pregnancy and STDs are concerned, prevention is better than cure, and self-confidence is good for your children's health.

Bully off!

Bullying constantly hits the headline, and many cases end in tragedy. Recent figures cite over a quarter of cases among under-12s, compared with about 10 per cent in the 13–16 age group, yet nearly everyone claims they've been bullied. People often don't realize that bullies and victims have one thing in common: low self-esteem.

What is bullying?

Few people admit to being bullies. Parents condemn it, but can't resist teasing their children – well, it's horribly funny when somebody completely over-reacts. Empathy is vital; one person's pinprick is somebody else's unbearable pain, and it does no good making excuses: 'It's just a joke.' Everybody has their own ideas about bullying, often based on what they had to put up with, e.g. gangs of lads beating up some poor kid. Increasingly, groups of girls are involved, even best friends; it can also be parents and teachers. Long-term effects also result from: extortion; 'borrowing' belongings or clothing, or ruining them; threatening gestures; pulling faces; insults; mockery; mimicry; malicious gossip; notes; graffiti; exclusion. Matters are exacerbated because onlookers and victims, even adults, are too scared or disheartened to speak out.

Villains, victims and self-esteem

The insecure are often irritatingly restless, acting or responding inappropriately. Bullies tend to be loud, rude, cocky and aggressive; victims are withdrawn, giggly, silly, over-eager. But if only we were talented, clever, or good-looking (preferably all three), then of course, we'd be happy. Bullies spoil things for others, so they always come out on top, while victims sabotage things for themselves, because they're downtrodden. Bullies believe they can do what they want and have anything they want (but are never satisfied). They blame everybody else, despising people who like them because it's based on fear. They cannot face up to guilt, which makes them even angrier. Picking on other people makes them feel better, gives them a sense of power – besides, they were asking for it. Victims know they can't get anything right and don't deserve anything (they can't enjoy things). They blame themselves for everything, assuming people must say they like them out of pity. Being picked on by the minute goes to prove it's their fault.

Signs of bullying

- Changes in attitude: frightened of walking to school or getting the school bus. Indifferent about schoolwork. Obsessive: cleanliness, possessions, punctuality. Doesn't look forward to or enjoy family treats. 'In a world of their own'; inattentive, withdrawn, evasive.
- Changes in behaviour: truanting or going missing; takes longer to come home; uses different routes or insists on lifts; comes up with stories, lies, unlikely excuses. Acts unreasonably or aggressively; nervous; babyish; thumb-sucking; nail-biting.
- Health: claims to be ill first thing (or won't get out of bed); ends up in sick bay or sent home. Loss of appetite, sudden dieting or overeating (stolen dinner money); stammering; bedwetting; sleeplessness; nightmares.
- Results (obvious signs should always be investigated): keeps borrowing money; pockets loose change, 'forgets' to hand it over, or 'loses' it; shoplifting. Won't go to school; won't go out or call for friends or go to usual places out of school. Frequently tearful; over-reacts. Unexplained cuts, bite marks, scratches, bruises; missing, damaged or 'loaned' possessions: clothes, books, schoolwork, bag, sports equipment.
- Keeps talking about, threatens, or attempts suicide.

Accentuate the positive

Even if parents can't give as much attention as children need, they can help them take more pride in themselves. Entrust them with straightforward tasks, giving them responsibility, and credit where it's due, even for the little things. Offer a suitable reward in advance, maybe a few sweets – although both bullies and victims will regard it as bribery. Avoid sarcasm, emotional blackmail, labelling or 'teaching them a lesson'; bullying the bully. Wrongdoing should be punished, though attempting to apportion blame wastes time; accusing the bully doesn't help victims as much as trying to solve the situation. Sometimes, bullies (and accomplices) don't understand the harm they're doing, or how much it affects victims. They must be made aware that people won't stand for it.

Equally, encourage victims to stand up for themselves. So-called 'provocative victims' persist in using a manner of talking and behaving which gets them into trouble. Confident people are rarely bullied, though their own behaviour may come close to bullying. Watch out for signs to circumvent potential problems: outbursts of bad behaviour, sulks and displays of bad temper. Otherwise, try to be non-committal; responses such as pleading, coaxing or anger 'reward' this kind of behaviour, proof that it does the trick; like publicity, attention for something bad is better than none.

Approaching the school

All schools should have an anti-bullying policy, including areas where teachers have to deal with aggressive parents, but it's said 22 per cent of children's complaints go no further. Over half the boys bullied do tell their parents, around three out of five girls. If the school's unhelpful, parents could make sure everyone locally knows about it, seeking support from the Citizens' Advice Bureau, the church, Samaritans etc. Having raised the matter with the Head, if dissatisfied with the outcome, the next step is the Board of Governors, via their parent representative. After that: the local Director of Education, local MP, town or county councillor, then the Secretary of State for Education.

Bullying as a criminal offence

This ranges from verbal assault (requires at least one witness; in a series of incidents, videos, cameras or tape recorders provide proof – and a deterrent) to Grievous Bodily Harm (GBH): broken bones; severe bruising; hospital treatment, or even GBH With Intent: serious injury which may result in death. All physical assaults should be reported; take photos of the injuries and keep records of medical treatment. Ask to speak to the Officer in Charge and a charge sheet will be made out, sometimes enough in itself to deter the attacker, and help the victim, showing steps have been taken.

Cigarettes and alcohol abuse

Admonish your children about drugs, and their immediate response is to ask you about cigarettes and alcohol. Or tranquillizers, the most widely prescribed drug.

Many of us like the odd drink, or need something to perk us up or calm us down, though fewer people now are smokers. Most youngsters reckon having recourse to these things is on a par with taking drugs – they're all as bad for your health.

Addictions

Even back in 1986, it was calculated that more money went on illegal drugs than on food. Currently, it's reported that nearly half the children tested in any secondary school showed traces of drugs. Don't kid yourself about expensive habits; heroin or cocaine don't come cheap, but pocket money is sufficient to purchase ecstasy, LSD, pot or speed. What most parents know about drugs could be written on the back of a postage stamp, but teenagers do experiment. However, with about 1 per cent of the entire population being classed as addicts, they aren't all doomed.

The main difference between cigarettes and alcohol and drugs is that the first two are legal. Some addicts resort to violence and crime, but so do alcoholics. Smoking, in that sense, causes less harm, other than for those suffering the effects of passive smoking. And with things that make us feel good and look good, by golly, none of us are too concerned they aren't doing us much good.

Smoking

It's been claimed that cigarette manufacturers add chemicals to tobacco to make it more addictive and more palatable, in order to attract a younger market, i.e. replacing all those who die through smoking-related diseases. It was recently alleged the best way to stop youngsters from starting to smoke (it's harder to give up) is to concentrate on issues like filthy capitalism and exploitation, rather than the way it affects your looks or health reasons. As for girls taking up smoking to get thinner, it's more the case that giving up sometimes means a weight increase.

In the 1940s, well over three-quarters of the population smoked; it's now less than one-third. However, the percentage of 15-year-olds who smoke is about equivalent to the total of adult smokers. It takes only four cigarettes for about nine-tenths of people to become smokers;

when parents smoke, children are twice as likely to take it up, but four times as likely when siblings are smokers. With most young children being strongly anti-smoking, parents are apt to become complacent, reassured they'll never try cigarettes. More teenagers appear to be taking up smoking under the impression that it's easy to stop, largely through the advertising of the various products designed for that purpose. More dangerous is the belief that once you stop smoking, any health damage is soon reversed.

Call me irresponsible

Some parents actually contribute to their offspring's addictive behaviour because of the way they're seen coping under stress: avoiding responsibility by blaming others; making excuses to get out of awkward situations; repressing feelings or slumping into depression or anxiety. Do you believe the only way to conquer addictions is total prohibition, or pride yourself on moderation in all things (even if your idea of moderation is either generous or obsessive)? And when do you light up a cigarette or fix yourself a quick drink?

And what about being too impatient or over-protective? Children who aren't allowed to choose, whether clothes, toys or TV programmes, grow up to find it hard making decisions. Kept ignorant about drugs, etc, they're more in danger than being kept safe. Other problems: failing to teach children to be assertive; not bothering to learn enough to take note of warning signs; ignoring such signs, to avoid facing up to the problem; over-reacting with anger and threats: taking all the responsibility and blame; keeping it secret rather than asking for help. Few parents think alcohol is as bad as drugs, yet alcohol abuse kills more people than all drugs put together.

Tell-tale signs

Teenagers' fluctuating temperament means that intensity of behaviour or changes, e.g. in eating or sleeping habits, are taken for granted or pass unnoticed. Different patterns may indicate abuse: moodiness; lethargy or sudden bursts of energy; inability to concentrate; more stressed or over-reacting. Shiftiness, lying and secrecy to the point of obsession are indicators, as are physical signs: red blotchiness around the mouth or nose, pupils constricted or dilated. And more obvious signs: any kind of unusual materials or equipment; strange stains and smells; money or valuables going missing.

Alcohol: some facts and figures

In Ancient Greece, newly-weds under 30, of both sexes, were forbidden to drink, to ensure healthier children; and the Bible advises pregnant women not to drink; women are more at risk due to their physique. By the age of 12, the number of children who drink outnumber non-drinkers. About one-fifth of 13-year-old boys have been very drunk; half as many girls. Over three-quarters in the 16-plus age group are regular drinkers, and by 19, over 10 per cent of boys and 5 per cent of girls suffer from alcohol dependency.

They say alcohol is good for your health, and since most of us do feel better after a glass or two, it doesn't occur to people that alcohol is a depressant. Like most drugs, it's popular because it makes you feel relaxed, which stops you worrying, so then you feel more confident (for a time at least). But alcohol slows down reactions. There are more deaths from alcohol-related accidents than illness, accounting for about one-quarter of all patients. Each year, around 1,000 youngsters under 15 need emergency treatment for alcohol poisoning, a tenfold increase in past ten years. In one study, 50 per cent of head injuries resulted from people drinking, from accidents to assaults, and the majority of crime in pubs and clubs is due to alcohol, as are most stabbings and beatings. A quarter of the 13–17 age group gets into fights after drinking. That's also when well over three-quarters try pot for the first time, and twice as many girls have unprotected sex.

Few teenagers realize that alcohol has more effect on them, and more quickly, than adults. Parents can help by discussing relevant issues like drink driving, and agreeing some ground rules. These can also be applied to parties. Parents should also find out as much as they can about alcohol and its effects, including alco pops. Lager and ciders used to be regarded on a par with soft drinks but some brands now contain a lot more alcohol.

Drugs and substance abuse

Drugs and illegal substances could be divided into two: natural substances, like pot (which has both depressant and hallucinogenic properties; nicotine is both stimulant and sedative), and manmade (e.g. solvents), but they're usually classified in three types:

- depressants (alcohol; heroin; barbiturates and tranquillizers);
- stimulants (cocaine; ecstasy; amphetamines);
- hallucinogenics (LSD; magic mushrooms).

Recent figures show that at just over 40 per cent, pot is most popular amongst 16–29-year-olds. Amphetamines come next (about one-fifth), then LSD, magic mushrooms and ecstasy, around 10 per cent, with cocaine at approximately 6 per cent. Heroin is at the bottom: 1 per cent, but it's about 2 per cent for 13–14-year-olds, and 3 per cent of 15–16-year-olds. Over half the population has experimented with drugs (twice as common in men), and there's more use in singles of all ages, generally the very poor, the very rich and the newly rich.

Reasons to be cheerful . . .

All the substances above affect behaviour and attitude, and experimenting with them is mainly to feel good, or to avoid feeling bad. Motivation, being linked with youngsters' self-esteem, high or low, is paradoxical: rebellious or powerless, bored and depressed, or because it makes them feel free or secure.

It's the in-thing, with the ritual and being part of a group. To parents, drugs are a problem, but for children, they look like the solution to their problems, making them feel mature and in control. And they're easily obtained.

Telling tales

Popular myth has youngsters preyed on by conscienceless dealers, but it's mostly friends who introduce them to drugs. Some are put off simply because it's impossible to tell in advance what the effect will be. Those who do decide to experiment are convinced that they'll never end up addicted. Or seriously ill. Or dead. However, taking drugs like pot doesn't inevitably mean going on to harder drugs (smoking pot has been alleged to lead to smoking cigarettes, rather than vice versa). And parents are reluctant to concede that drug use is often recreational, on a par with other social habits like smoking and drinking. This restricts them to warning children about risk and illegality (see pp. 93–5).

When users contain the habit, soft drugs don't necessarily lead to dependency. But there is a fine line between use and abuse, being sensible and becoming out of control; the following are rough guidelines:

- sticking to occasional use and small amounts, always from the same source;
- purchasing small quantities, avoiding getting into debt;
- never changing drugs or mixing them with others;
- not using in public or with strangers;
- not dealing.

Reasons to be careful

- Mixing drugs and drink is one short cut to getting high, but it's easy to overdose with barbiturates.
- Magic mushrooms: 12 different kinds, may be confused with something poisonous.
- Using needles increases the risk of HIV and blood poisoning; if that leads to gangrene, amputation may be necessary.

Once dependent, addiction can follow:

- physical: taking drugs to avoid withdrawal symptoms such as nausea, insomnia, sweating, etc;
- psychological because it gives you a buzz.

When you need more drugs, you need more money to pay for them, hence the link with crime; using drugs affects your ability to work and to find work. It's also time-consuming, all your energy concentrated on the next fix, finding the wherewithal and supplies. The effects start to wear off faster; amphetamines last three to four hours, but for cocaine/crack, it's about 15 to 20 minutes.

When does taking drugs become a problem? When it's the first thing you think of on waking up. When it's the only thing you think of all day, every day.

Prevention or cure

Parents can take steps to adjust the odds, making their children's friends welcome and getting to know them. At times, you'll feel the house is not your own (cupboards always bare, sink full of dishes), but take it as a compliment that your children still feel at home, even if they're always complaining. If they were that fed up, they'd be hanging around street corners. Stick to some basic guidelines, house rules to be respected by friends and family. Reassure your children that when they go out, you'll come and pick them up if need be, whatever time or place or reason (no questions asked). In awkward situations, when reluctant to say 'no', it's useful to be able to blame parents for not letting you do something or go somewhere.

Toughing it out

Parents are quick to overestimate their children's abilities, particularly intelligence ('If he really put his mind to it, you know, that lad could go far . . .'), and to play down any problems, eager to accept promises and excuses – 'Not my child'. There's little point in assuming that addiction is down to having a weak character, and of course they could stop if they wanted. It's a lot more complex. Youngsters are past masters at divide and conquer, playing mother off against dad and vice versa, but parents must stick together. When a child decides to quit, the situation does not immediately improve; many parents find this difficult, particularly as it often takes several attempts. Addicts feel empty and at a loss, unable to settle to anything, with such habits being a time-consuming activity. But once they've got this far, the fun's gone out of it, so they tend to persevere. What turns them around isn't always their parents' efforts; it could be a change of environment, getting a new job, or meeting somebody new.

It's generally agreed that an addict has to touch bottom before they can ask for help, and you could try accelerating the drop by making things uncomfortable: no laundry, meals or lifts. However, if life's that miserable, they may resort to drugs for relief, so maintain a balance. You need to learn to avoid nagging, and trust them again, showing that you do. Assure your children that although you don't like what they've done, you'll always love them.

Reasons to be hopeful

Once children make up their mind to quit, there are plenty of means of support, offering advice and information: counselling, rehabilitation centres, self-help groups. Parents can confide in friends, seek their support. They face another challenge – tough love, refusing to provide the means to support their habit: no hand-outs of any kind, for any reason: losing a job, their beloved, the best chance they're ever, ever likely to have. And refuse to lay blame, or to feel guilt. Just say no. Concentrate on restoring their belief in themselves, that they will get through.

Parents need to ensure that children accept responsibility for their own actions, make up their own mind. Think about the way your parents treated you, and how you'd have liked them to treat you. Listen to what your children have to say, and, when requested, offer help and express your opinion. Make sure you all know the facts, avoid mistakes and myths. Think positive, about their achievements, and your own. Equally, be honest about your mistakes, something parents and children always have in common, though the latter often remain unaware of it. Spend time with them, working on chores together (redecorating the bathroom) or sharing a treat (visiting the cinema). Make the most of opportunities to discuss issues, e.g. picking up a prescription. What's their school's policy? Talk about what they're being taught.

Parents themselves have decisions to make: where do you draw the line? Some things, in the long run, aren't that important. In discussion with your children, make sure they know exactly what and where the bottom line is. If they come home with their ears pierced, to accusations of looking like a tart and dire warnings about hellfire and damnation, what's left to say if you find the police on your doorstep?

Crime and punishment

With children fast approaching adolescence, they're going to get up to all sorts. Don't bury your head in the paper (the headlines only make you feel worse), study the facts.

Bad news

About half of all crime is committed by people aged 10–21, all but around one-tenth being vandalism and theft (cars, property, break-ins, muggings). The number of women offenders is rising, and most are in the 15–20 age group: usually for fraud, theft, handling stolen goods and shoplifting. About 50 per cent of them are believed to have a child under 16, about one-third a child under five. Over half claimed the reason was lack of money; other reasons were: mixing with the wrong crowd; supporting their children; drink or drugs; family problems; unemployment. By the age of 40, less than 10 per cent of all women have a conviction compared with over one-third of men.

And the good news?

Over two-thirds of juvenile crime is committed by about 5 per cent of offenders, so the majority of youngsters are not wrongdoers, and nearly four-fifths of those cautioned don't get into trouble again. They aren't necessarily heading for a life of crime. But what makes them do it in the first place? When a child wanders from the straight and narrow, parents start blaming themselves, and though most of us are prone to be lax about some things, what if you're always boasting how you fiddle your expenses?

The reasons why

With any kind of crime, up comes the nature/nurture argument. Since most teenage tearaways appear cocky, people generally assume it's due to excess confidence, rather than a lack of it. Society insists that when an individual is described as evil, this must be innate, because of their genes. It cannot possibly be due to environmental factors, not even the fabled broken home. That would mean we're all at risk: given certain circumstances, anybody would be evil.

One reason boys are more inclined to delinquent behaviour (whether joyriding or stealing money to play on fruit machines or buy lottery tickets) is said to result from being less closely supervised than girls. It's also an extreme way of attention-seeking, a means of expressing strong emotions like anger, when unable to do so verbally.

Plus excess testosterone, the need for the buzz of excitement, and a means of acting out their sexual impulses; boys are believed to be more likely to get into trouble in the months before their first sexual experience.

Factors

Like parents, teachers reckon they can spot trouble at an early age, and doom-laden prophecies are often borne out. As for addictive behaviour, nobody knows why some people are more prone than others. Many recovering alcoholics insist they daren't take another drink because they'll be back to square one, but there's little evidence of 'addictive personality', handy though it would be to explain away criminal tendencies. Maybe some kind of syndrome or disease? It is now thought possible that there is a genetic predisposition, e.g. for alcoholism or gambling, which seems to run in families. Stress, as usual, is brought into it, and now gender, with young girls turning more to crime. Other motives are boredom and frustration, thrill-seeking, pleasure and curiosity.

Poverty and class are amongst the external factors, although juvenile delinquents come from all kinds of families. They are believed to be adversely influenced by poor family relationships and educational problems. Peer pressure plays a part, and sometimes other causes are cited, including religious, mystical or occult experiences.

The law and drugs

Some parents have gone to the police and shopped their children, and some have gone out shopping to buy them drugs. Few people know how they'll react in any situation until they find themselves slap bang in the middle of it but both parents and children should be aware of the legal position. Growing illegal substances is an offence, as is supplying, and that's not simply selling drugs, but sharing them or handing them back to somebody. Possession is another flexible term; if parents unearth illegal drugs in the home, technically it's an offence to flush them down the toilet. When handing them in to the police, it's deemed wiser to suggest they were found in the street. All those sharing a joint are considered guilty, and 'possession' applies when leaving drugs somewhere for collection later on, or even if the substance turns out to be harmless, e.g. buying pills at a club, which are actually headache tablets. Having any equipment related to drugs is not illegal, but it would be regarded as evidence.

It's also illegal for parents to allow the production or supplying of drugs in their home. Although allowing the use of pot or opium is technically an offence, the police are unlikely to prosecute, nor do they in the case of other drugs, even if you knew your children were using them, or allowed them to do so. If you decide to inform the police, unless it is a matter of dealing or dangerous drugs, it results in a caution rather than a criminal record. Nonetheless, your children should know that it could be several years before any conviction is removed from the record, and would be taken into consideration for any further offences. It also affects their chances of employment and of going abroad.

Punishment

In law, currently, up to the age of 10, children are regarded as being unable to form 'criminal intention'. From 10 to 14, they must be shown to know their actions are wrong, and from 14 onwards, they are treated as an adult, although 14–18-year-olds are dealt with in a juvenile court.

Police procedure (stop and search)

Under-18s may be stopped by the police, e.g. on suspicion of having alcohol on them. They must give their name and address (and manners maketh life a little easier; be polite, even when you've done nothing wrong). Likewise, the police must give a reason for questioning and searching them (outer clothing and bag, if suspected of possessing drugs); an 'arrestable offence' means they are suspected of: possessing stolen goods, or an offensive weapon, or have the means to commit a crime (having somebody else's purse or wallet).

Part 4 High life: suggestions for improving self-confidence

Assert yourself

Putting what you learn about assertion into practice is rarely an overnight success. That first big step is enormous because you anticipate anger, ridicule, tears, threats. Any one of these is often the initial reaction, which is very discouraging. But it's worth it because to improve self-confidence, we need to be assertive. It's a vital skill, yet many parents don't encourage it in children, or even show enthusiasm when the latter are pleased with what they've done, in case they get too big for their boots. Anybody who expresses quiet satisfaction is liable to be considered big-headed (usually by those with low self-esteem). Assertive people know how to communicate needs, in a reasonable and straightforward manner which shows respect for others.

Asking for it

Trouble is, being assertive is confused with being aggressive. Ideally, requests, etc. should be made without bluster, over-apologising or rambling, with no need for capitulation or manipulation – certainly no veiled threats, intimidation or hurting others with name-calling or abuse. Those who don't ask, don't get, but it depends who's doing the asking and how they go about it. Some people always seem to get their own way, but we usually divide into three groups: aggressive, passive, and assertive.

- Aggressive behaviour: deep-seated belief that you hit them before they hit you, because you're the most important person, and besides, it's tough out there.
- Passive personality: stuck with this line of thinking: well, I suppose I deserve to get hit. Just goes to prove how scary it is out there, and that I'm completely unimportant.
- Assertive: reflects a more reasonable outlook: what's the point of getting violent about anything, when it's usually fine out there, and I'm as important as anybody else?

Few people would dream of thinking that last phrase, let alone voice it out loud; the world would soon bring you down a peg. Yet it does no harm to show pride in your achievements; calmly stating a fact is not the same as showing off. People with low self-esteem are prone to boasting, needing others' approval to validate what they've accomplished. Confident people content themselves with knowing they've done well.

Helping children to be assertive

We can assert ourselves when necessary, e.g. protect our children, and there are courses for such skills, but it isn't difficult to learn them yourself, then teach your children. You'll both have ample opportunity to practise them: make requests; say no; disagree; give and receive compliments; accept criticism and rejection. The ability to convey confidence makes you feel more confident, and that leads to success, which in turn, gives you confidence: a victorious circle.

> Anna has led a quiet life and tends to get uptight about travelling, particularly long train journeys. She manages to relax by being as elegant as possible and behaving like somebody famous (yet gracious) attempting to pass incognito.

Few people like a cocky child, but it's as likely to be a sign of insecurity as over-confidence. Children who are full of themselves are unaware of their faults, or blithely disregard them. They're liable to make more mistakes, failing to learn from them, as well as endangering themselves (and others) through the inability to foresee consequences. Having good, nice, kind children means life runs smoothly for parents, but that's no guarantee life will run smoothly for them. You can make it much easier by encouraging them to offer ideas and opinions, paying attention to what they say. Move on to constructive criticism, steeling yourself for adverse comment about the clothes you planned on wearing to sports day. Your reaction demonstrates that criticism can be useful rather than destructive; rejecting something is not the same as wholesale rejection of somebody.

Fight for your rights

Everybody has rights: asking for what you want or for help; saying no; complaining; changing your mind; making mistakes; expressing ideas or feelings; keeping secrets; being proud of yourself. Help children to remember this, and to feel more secure, e.g. by designing a poster. Remind them that they are not being selfish or stupid, even if that's what the reaction of others suggests. It all helps reassure them, whether they feel there's something they really can't do without or they've cause for complaint.

Making requests

Nagging, wheedling or demanding children are exasperating when they should explain things clearly. Ask for something simply, politely and directly; openings like 'I know you're not going to agree, but . . .'

deserve a swift riposte – inevitably no. Avoid requests escalating into a row using simple repetition: 'Can I have my CD back please?' If requests are refused, compromise avoids a winners and losers situation.

Paying compliments

We all like some acknowledgement we've done well, preferably to our face rather than via a third party. Something specific, rather than a general comment like 'That's nice' shows true appreciation; a few kind words are more effective than fulsome rhetoric. Trying to cheer somebody up with a compliment won't always work, but even people who find it hard to respond graciously can smile. That's often all that's needed.

Criticism

Children dread the phrase 'Yes, it's very nice, but . . .', while parents dread the outcome if they don't offer a helping hand. It's our duty, after all. Another dodgy balancing act, encouraging them to think for themselves and produce something to a good enough standard, without totally undermining their confidence. Mistakes tend to catch the eye but need pointing out tactfully; the immediate response is assuming that having done something stupid means you're stupid. It doesn't improve matters if it is the result of carelessness.

Only trying to help

Few books on self-esteem give much advice about this situation; trial and error is the best description. Some children appreciate you trying to help, but others are mortified that it's not 100 per cent perfect. They may flatly refuse to listen, storm off, or refuse to make any further attempts.

One practical solution can be hard for parents to carry out (especially those who see their children's achievements as reflecting on them): offer specific praise about the good bits, i.e. 'I love the colours you've chosen' but NOT 'Goodness, darling, that is clever! Such a pity you didn't . . .'. Harder still: ask permission to offer further comments. Any reluctance, don't say a word. Or drop hints. It's not the end of the world if they receive five out of ten for their own efforts, even when you know damn well if they'd only listened to you, it would have been nine and a half at least.

Offering constructive criticism

Even young children can learn to observe basic rules in giving and receiving criticism. Show consideration for other people's feelings;

start with a positive comment, i.e. good news, bad news. Providing it's clear you've given the matter thought, rather than speaking on impulse (or snapping at them), people are more prepared to listen. They're also more likely to take criticism on board and modify their behaviour if it benefits them. Siblings 'borrow' things, knowing what the answer will be, even to a polite request. But the person agreeing to the loan, owed a favour, is ahead on points.

Watch your timing: avoid criticizing anyone in public; being humiliated is no guarantee that behaviour won't be repeated. When mortified, do you even take in what's said? It's pointless offering criticism to somebody who isn't paying attention. And stick to one thing at a time. Chuck everything in, you won't make your point. Even if disposing of only one grievance, be gracious; no need to make them feel worse with choice of words, tone of voice, patronizing smile or body language.

On the receiving end

That was the easy bit; nobody enjoys being criticized, but there's a big difference depending on how it's doled out, and how you deal with it. When children openly criticize you, they're apt to be blunt. Suppose you spent all afternoon experimenting with something different for dinner? But when you make their favourite cake, despairing that it never looks like the ones on TV, if it tastes good, every crumb's demolished, along with your doubts.

Stay calm. Deep breaths and a conscious effort to relax help you cope; we're all prone to over-react when criticized, feeling under attack. Be positive. It may be harsh, it may be necessary – it won't be pleasant. But if criticism is meant to be helpful, pay attention. One reason we try to avoid repeating mistakes is to escape such consequences. Be philosophical. Everybody makes mistakes; nobody's perfect. Do something bad and it makes you feel bad, but that doesn't mean you're a bad person.

Take your time. Criticism often leads to conflict; we immediately want to put our own view across or justify ourselves. Jumping in or rushing to conclusions can land us in a bigger mess. Always ask questions where necessary. If what has been said is unfair or upsets you, or you need to think or work out how best to respond, try stonewalling: calmly agree, repeatedly, that the other person may have a point.

This sometimes floors them to the extent that they give up straightaway, but if not, keep going; they'll get fed up before you do. It may feel odd, but helps you cope with awkward situations, e.g.

being criticized in front of other people. No matter what the cause for complaint, if you stay calm and pleasant, it's the person doing the criticizing who looks bad. Besides, they could be over-reacting because of a bad mood, or habitually criticize, or they're mean and spiteful. Accepting that the other person could be right is not the same as accepting the blame. Much easier to do when you're assertive, and once it becomes habit, so does self-confidence.

Nice gesture: how body language improves children's self-esteem

You never get a second chance to make a good first impression, and non-verbal communication or body language is remarkably revealing. People know instantly whether somebody is confident; when insecure, they try to look inconspicuous: head lowered, no eye contact, shoulders slumped. Knowledge of body language often comes in useful; doctors learn a lot about their patients' ailments from gestures; a pointing finger indicates some kind of stabbing pain. However, there are myths about the subject: it doesn't make you transparent, nor can you use it to fool or manipulate others. Everything depends on the situation, the people and other signals; each particular gesture doesn't always have a single meaning. Arms crossed tightly over the chest? That's for protection; are you angry or anxious? Or feeling the cold?

Everyone tends to use one particular method of thinking and learning: visual; auditory; kinaesthetic; digital. If somebody is teaching visually (diagrams, drawing, etc.), it won't work very well with kinaesthetic pupils (i.e. hands-on experience). Students always make lecture notes, but that's more use to those who learn digitally. Body language is a powerful means for parents to help youngsters who lack confidence, even from an early age, enabling them to understand children better ('What's up then?' 'Nothing, honest') It also means they can communicate better with their children and show them how to communicate with others.

Wake-up time

There are four states of consciousness which exhibit different body language: uptime; downtime; trance; sleep. 'Trance', i.e. somebody lost in thought, is not as profound as 'sleep', whilst 'downtime' is lighter than trance, to process information, i.e. reflection, though it rather implies feeling miserable. The opposite is 'uptime', when you're alert, using your senses. Body language enables you to change states. To improve concentration, switch from uptime to downtime: lower your head, looking down to the centre of the body and shut your eyes; breathe in slowly through your nose to a count of five heartbeats, ditto, breathing out through the mouth. Repeat five times.

Conflicting emotions

From babies less than 24 hours old, children model themselves on their parents, and can copy them in a fraction of a second. They sense you're uptight because it shows: posture (stiffness); movements (disjointed, repetitive); expression; eyes; voice (high and rapid). You're more distracted (downtime), controlling the need to speak out by clenching jaw and mouth, comforting yourself by patting your face or body.

In a family crisis, children adopt different strategies: intervening, ignoring or modelling. They copy tense postures, behave more aggressively or become clingy, intervening by offering comfort or demanding attention. Or they attempt to ignore what's going on, avoiding others and shutting themselves in. It's obvious to a child when parents have trouble showing emotion, and they're unconsciously absorbing something they're too young to fully understand.

Second that emotion

Children can be taught early on to name the emotions which others display: describing it, then explaining, e.g. facial expression, particularly the mouth and eyes (safer sticking to TV rather than real life; children have loud voices). They can try expressing their own feelings, maybe on a scale of one to ten. Most of the basic emotions are experienced in a child's tummy, e.g. nausea (disgust), heaviness (sadness), butterflies (fear or happiness). Each is exhibited through facial expression, posture, breathing and skin colour, but whereas breathing quickens in all cases, skin grows pale (except with happiness), turning redder if angered, and if a surprise turns out to be something nice.

With mixed emotions, gestures are contradictory: movement and expression, eyes and mouth, or actions and words. Confusing for parents, it's incomprehensible to children; when frightened by their feelings, they then become angry.

> George loves animals and is so excited about his first trip to the zoo, he can't stop talking about it. Once there, though, he alarms his parents by hanging onto them for dear life: it's all so big and crowded, and the animals are loud and smelly. Safe inside the café, and offered his favourite ice cream, he bursts into tears.

Parents can help with physical support, and ease children's distress by explaining that what they're feeling is natural. Talk it through until all emotions are dealt with, and body language is no longer contradictory.

When children suppress emotions, they block out their feelings, closing themselves off and becoming still and quiet so they won't reveal what they're thinking. If overwhelmed by emotion, the result is a tantrum or a panic attack. Both can be dealt with by learning to recognize the signs; calm them down by 'matching': copying posture, gesture or expression reassures them. Avoid a crisis by controlling emotion through physical movement, e.g. taking slow, deep breaths and getting them into a more upright position, or standing up and moving around.

Children can psych themselves up when they need more confidence to use their skills, e.g. in sport: recalling an occasion when full of confidence, in as much detail as possible, remembering how they felt; simultaneously, making themselves as tall as possible: tensing and relaxing limbs, grinning, then relaxing, widening eyes, staring straight ahead and repeating some confidence-boosting phrase like 'Go for it!'; finally, bouncing on the spot for a moment until they feel the surge of energy – and do it.

Social skills

Children soon learn they have to get on with one another, but not how to go about it, and there are distinct differences between lonely children and those who want to be alone. Watching them, it's apparent that the former are more hesitant and don't move much, looking around to check up on the other children. Children enjoying their own company are relaxed, engrossed in what they're doing. Those trying to appear confident avoid looking at anyone, to keep up appearances. Different ways of moving are also revealing: smooth, uncoordinated, unduly relaxed, respectively.

Children in groups adopt particular roles, and body language is a dead giveaway: the Scapegoat hunches up as if trying to be unobtrusive, while the Bighead is loud, taking up loads of space. Other roles include: Baby or Mini-parent, Mummy's boy/Daddy's girl, Clown, Tomboy.

Some grow out of this naturally, others need help to mature, i.e. to become more confident. Each group obviously has a leader; with teenage boys, the one in charge keeps particular friends close by, others at a distance, though all members vie to bag a place nearest to him. Always first to speak, everyone pays attention to him, and when he doles out favours, the recipients show off to the others.

Conflict seems neverending in group situations, but doesn't always mean a fight; threatening may resolve it, when the opponent backs down. Or both start losing interest and cool off. They may also regress, changing from threatening to wanting to be taken care of, or simply submit, 'playing dead' so the opponent leaves them alone.

Yes, and no

Conversation is a social skill, which not all adults successfully master, but parents can practise the following with children to help them feel more confident with others:

- signals for taking turns: a pause or a glance cue in both participants; lifting your hand indicates you want to speak;
- eye contact and nodding at important points or intervals show you're paying attention;
- speeding up your nods and looking away indicate you've had enough;
- shifting position, less eye contact and longer pauses bring conversations to an end.

Some people have a gift for moving in closer, exhibiting rejection or anger, getting their own way by using more threatening behaviour. Saying no requires appropriate body language or it's undermined, leading to mixed messages. Don't smile, laugh nervously or speak quickly; no leaning forward, touching or speaking softly, and looking away. Show you mean what you say: stay relaxed, but step back, face the other person, maintain eye contact, speak evenly. A slight shake of the head reinforces refusal. To be able to say no, making it clear that you mean it, is a sign of healthy self-esteem.

Younger children I: story-telling

Not the same as teaching children to read, though equally important – but avoid making them learn to read, or listen to you reading. If the former is a problem, instead of sticking with Joan and John, try non-fiction. Young children are usually passionate about something, from dinosaurs to computers, and there are always plenty of books on the various subjects. Let them choose; better for them to be interested and improve their abilities than for you to select something suitable. As Einstein said, imagination is more important than knowledge.

Speaking volumes

Many parents think they do well managing a few minutes each bedtime; the ritual is calming and helps children enjoy books. Some have pretty gruesome tastes, and stories create a safe environment to explore such feelings, but don't encourage nightmares. Experiment with the more thrilling stuff during the daylight hours.

Stories evoke emotions in everybody, though we often are unaware of how and why we feel certain things; they can penetrate the subconscious, literally making us feel better, healing us. That's the value of escapism, alongside being rapt in a book. It rescues children, in a sense, makes them feel better about themselves, particularly tales mirroring their own situation, helping them feel less isolated. Being secure makes it easier to prepare for difficulties, and they learn to empathize with others, to understand symbolism: things are not always what they seem. Books are useful to parents as a metaphor, making it easier to bring up issues such as bullying, rather than through confrontation.

Daytime activities related to story-telling

Listening to stories has a practical value, requiring children to sit still and to focus. Some seem incapable of staying put, and need a lot more practice than others, but can be encouraged to learn to concentrate using play activities involving stories:

- making up an album or scrapbook;
- writing a letter or a diary;
- 'show and tell' (learning presentation skills is good for children inclined to be shy).

They can also retell stories or use a different viewpoint; tell their own stories or draw them; list the traits of the main characters and compare them with their own.

Is it just my imagination?

The mind plays tricks: your worst enemy or your best friend. It isn't actual situations which bring about stress, but our perception of them; with no limit to the imagination, no wonder it runs away with you. When used positively, though, it proves incredibly powerful. Practice helps it counteract such effects, an antidote to stress, by guiding you consciously, via language, stories and imagery, to reassess your values; positive emotions, like compassion, humour, etc. are encouraged, confidence improved.

Story-telling is form of celebration, traditionally taking place on special occasions, from weddings to Hallowe'en. Take heart from the fact that myths, legends and stories go back centuries in every culture, having always had therapeutic value (if not that description). They endure because there's always something to learn from them.

Useful themes

Even if you don't care for the moral of the story, seek out books for the following:

- Developing self-awareness: helps children to understand emotions and learn to be at peace with themselves, looking inwards rather than outwards, seeking instant gratification.
- Managing stress: encourage the half-full glass philosophy, along with perseverance. Aim to alter perception, to control responses and avoid brooding. In awkward situations, map out what's happened, what could happen, what's likely to result, how it can be dealt with. Relax with visualization, composing a script to reach your place in the sun. Adapt it for your children; relating it to them in a soothing voice enables them to concentrate more, helping them learn to relax.
- Using the imagination: collect pictures of things they like and stick them in a scrapbook; design a ladder to show what's required to achieve goals. Daydreaming about a rosy future relaxes you, and can help realize dreams and ambitions.
- Counting your blessings: and acting upon them. Being appreciated makes us feel good, and confident. Children can make a list or build up a collage.
- Caring for others is a common motif: when you care about yourself, it becomes natural to care about others, from family to the local community to globally.
- Making up your own story: as a joint family effort or take turns,

relating anecdotes or retelling memoirs. A popular theatre device is using something like a stick; whoever holds it, has the floor and shouldn't be interrupted.

When you think about it, most adult conversation consists of story-telling, from 'what happened to me at the shops', to 'you'll never believe what I found when scuba-diving.' Conversations with our children aren't always pleasurable experiences, and when they consist largely of instruction and correction, won't do much for their confidence.

Younger children II: improving confidence with games

Ask a bunch of toddlers something, they're nearly all eager to come up with the answer, and they can't wait to show their parents everything they've made. Once at school, children soon become modest to the point of invisibility; few make a show of hands. Past the egocentric stage, they need more encouragement; the big problem with being out in the world is that you're more open to comparison. When this appears odious, self-esteem suffers.

The kids are all right

Confidence means accepting the bad points with the good. Appreciate that, like all individuals, you are unique, and need to make the best of yourself: in what you do, how you are, the way you behave and treat others. Positive self-image encourages people to take risks, to learn and thus move on. Children need plenty of feedback, reassurance that what they do, and what they are, is just fine. Parents need to understand them, allowing them to express emotion, even vent feelings, without contradiction. In the heat of passion, we all burst out how we hate something. How do parents respond? Whether it's something different served up at breakfast or something mean served up anytime by a sibling, we tell our children: 'Don't be so silly.' No need to investigate, or try and solve any problems. Children should know that their parents are listening, even if they can't always make it better.

Is your inner child coming out to play?

The family which plays together, stays together. Sounds silly? A bit of fun does nobody any harm, and relaxation is good for us; chanting and songs get the creative side of the brain going. Some people take games very seriously, but it isn't a matter of competing. Games can be played in pairs or as a team effort, and the latter shows you how to work together, tackling strengths and weaknesses. Match the right game to the right time, place and mood:

- peaceful
- energetic
- outside
- in the car.

Most have variations, making them more interesting and easier to learn.

Fun and games

Nominate a day dedicated to one person, to choose what everybody does; for the reticent, it's more comfortable on birthdays. Or mark an occasion, a turning point like starting school, each family member offering praise for certain accomplishments. The child could say what he's most pleased about, but if he's embarrassed (or any of you), get into the habit of complimentary behaviour by using the imagination: the first Martian to have a no. 1 hit. Whether for something real or imagined, praise makes us feel good, though people with low self-esteem shrug it off or put it down to luck.

Feelings

Turn negatives into positives by compiling a list of the child's particular qualities: good-tempered, kind to small, furry animals, etc. Again, if too, too embarrassing, list negative characteristics (mean, jealous, etc.), then alter to the opposite. Children can start learning to deal with their emotions: think of various objects, then say how they feel about them and why: ice cream van, frogs. They could go on to talk about things which make them happy or sad, or parents can introduce variation by suggesting that they say the same sentence in different ways: surprised or bored, or act it out, e.g. pretending to be scared.

Senses

Parents think there's a time and place for daydreaming, but it is relaxing, and enables children to take in what's happening around them, like the 'Makes sense' game: 'When I hear a whistle, I feel ... ?'; 'When I smell the coffee, I feel ... ?' Other suggestions to learn to make the most of all the senses:

- Sound: hide something in a room; instead of saying hot or cold, hum loudly or quietly.
- Sight: send the child outside, then alter something; obvious (moving furniture) or subtle (removing an earring).
- Touch: put items into a bag and let them feel inside.
- Smell/taste: something distinctive (lemon, chips) which the child can make up stories about, or you can tell them about.

Just using a bit of common sense, and all these could become popular family pastimes, especially the last one.

Taking it all too literally

Healthy self-esteem harmonizes heart and mind, so that thoughts and emotions co-exist peacefully. Whether thoughts flicker past or hang round like black clouds obscuring everything, we don't usually register that they're in the form of images. With adults forever gloomily playing the 'What if . . .' record, children learn bad habits, always anticipating things going wrong, and getting the blame. A conscious effort to communicate more positive images, even when it's hard to look on the bright side of life, makes a big difference. We kid ourselves our children are too young to suffer from stress, but you can see the signs, even in toddlers.

It's because adults speak metaphorically that they remain unaware children are taking them literally; even when children are old enough to understand such common expressions as 'it's driving me mad', they still absorb negative messages. Abusive language, like repressed feelings, leads to physical ailments, hence our polite description of infuriating people being 'a pain in the neck'. Once parents habitually turn negatives into positives, communicating it to their children, they soon get the message:

> Jill's mother is watching her climbing a tree, every instinct urging her to yell: 'Will you be careful up there! You're going to fall and hurt yourself!' She manages to restrain yourself, calling out encouragement: 'Go on, you're doing fine!'

Confidence engendered in the child helps guarantee success. Doubt invariably leads to clumsiness, and then, more than likely, accidental damage.

Older children I: positive thinking

Never mind children, parents often fail to understand that self-esteem is based on a set of extremely potent thoughts, which give rise to emotions. When past experience has been largely negative, the inevitable result is lack of confidence. However, once determined to improve matters, it can take about a month to learn to adopt a more positive outlook, by being able to change your mind. Remember the old saying: 'mind over matter'? To improve self-esteem, remember: when you don't mind, it no longer matters, i.e. concentrate on accentuating the positive, and get rid of negative thoughts.

> Donna often finds her mind runs away with her, anticipating disaster and making her thoroughly miserable. What helps her to be more rational is spotting the old cartoon showing somebody with the devil perched on one shoulder, an angel on the other. She uses that image as a reminder: heeding the latter helps you shut out your inner voice's doom-laden mutterings.

The mind is a wonderful thing, but we use only a fraction of our brain power, often wasting it. Our thoughts give rise to emotions, which when negative, last far longer than happiness. Even when joyful, there's a tinge of bitter-sweetness because we know it won't last; applying the same principle to our darkest moments makes them more bearable. Negative thoughts can use up to three-quarters of our energy, depleting us of the motivation to do something about it. Learning to control your thoughts means they no longer have power over you; the right thoughts get the right results.

Divided between left and right

It may be fanciful to picture the two halves of the brain struggling in some kind of mental civil war, but it's not that far-fetched, because they should complement each other; most of us favour one or other, but we all alternate. The left brain is predominant during the daytime, whilst the right brain gains power when we're relaxed, e.g. preparing for sleep. It's responsible for intuition and creativity, using pictures and senses rather than thoughts, and processes all kinds of information, seeing the link between cause and effect, without judgement or criticism. The left brain is what's at work when you're at work: logic and analysis, dealing with things like words and numbers. But one thing at a time; you can't talk and do something else, concentrating equally on both. Hence that awful hamster wheel effect: something upsets you and your mind spins round and round, brooding. Or it flits from one worry to the next, as if to pollinate them, making them spread and blossom. Take some practical steps: rather than leaving the whole lot unresolved, prioritize, then consider each problem thoroughly in turn until you come to some sort of conclusion.

Like a video machine with only one tape, the left brain constantly replays past experiences which have conditioned us, painful or pleasant. However, through relaxation into the alpha state, that presleep dreaminess (see p. 116), the right brain takes charge and calms the other side down, and, with practice, can reprogramme it. This helps you resolve problems and get rid of destructive thoughts, thinking more positively. Ideally, the right brain provides inspiration, the left brain carries it out.

Lack of confidence and fears emanate from the unconscious, revealing themselves in habits or patterns of behaviour, which lead to low self-esteem. We repress the most painful experiences. However, just as you can use a video without knowing how it works, you can also wipe out negativity, replacing it with something more positive. When making decisions, logically you rely on past experience (left brain), but can also approach it more intuitively (right brain), although this is riskier.

Parent and child

It's impossible to please the whole family all the time and in all situations. Everyone goes through phases, up one minute, down the next, getting on like a house on fire, hating each other's guts. However, when two people usually get on, it's worth analysing why that's the case, or asking their advice about what happens when they do argue, how they sort it out. Try and put yourself in the other person's shoes; with children, think back to when you had rows with your parents. Or, when you get into bed, concentrate on their good points, and relive your happiest times. Memories vividly conjure up feelings of happiness so next time you're likely to fall out, use that 'photo' to counteract annoyance and prevent rows escalating. Similarly, avoid having a negative view of children, or anticipating poor results by picturing them doing well. When you can encourage them all the more, they react better, and are likely to succeed. If you clearly assume they're going to fail, what do you think will happen?

Learning to recognize warning signs of stress helps avert it, if you're able to relax sufficiently right away; remembering 'a few of your favourite things' also makes children feel better. Accumulated tension has to be released to avoid damage, by letting off steam promptly; anything physical, particularly exercise, does the trick. Let yourself go, from cushion thumping to screaming and shouting, get it all out of your system. Tantrum? Maybe, but providing your children see the funny side, you all have a good laugh. Relieve any remaining tension with a massage or soaking in a bath; tending those parts where it most gets to you, e.g. neck or spine.

Conscious of success

Positive thoughts reach through to the unconscious, bringing about a reality which need no longer be in negative circumstances. The unconscious equates thoughts with actions; when we remember dreams they seem surreal, but while we're dreaming, it's all really happening. Visualization is important to bring about the results you want and so is reframing. This allows you to rewrite unhappy past experiences, and in viewing a positive outcome, ease guilt and any sense of failure. Parents can help children think well of themselves by teaching them affirmations, said out loud and written down. Not as easy as it sounds, it does take practice. It's also useful to identify faults, but for the purpose of improvement, not to prove somebody is a bad person.

When something upsets you, it results in about a hundred physical changes in less than a second. If this is your standard response to disapproval or aggression (rather than actually turning the corner and coming face to face with a shoal of piranha), tension is generated and stored, leading to psychological and physical problems. Once this way of responding is habit, you're no longer in control. When other people and negative thoughts have you in their power, confidence loses out.

Older children II: positive action

Healthy mind, healthy body, and vice versa. It's virtually impossible to feel good about yourself when you're always tired or run down, but when energy levels are high, it improves vitality. The better you feel, the more confident you become. Nor is energy devoted purely to sport and exercise, it's also mental, emotional and spiritual. All these areas should balance, but focusing on one can impinge on the others.

Coaching couch potatoes

Parents often reckon children wear them out; where does all that energy come from? It soon goes; by the age of 10, they spend more time sitting down than they do being active. About one-third of boys and half the number of girls don't even manage to do half an hour's physical activity each week. Parents should exercise their imagination, and get their offspring going:

- under-5s: a few minutes each day helps to develop basic physical skills: throwing and catching; stepping; trampolining;
- fives to 12s: basic movements: balancing; jumping; skipping; running and swimming;
- twelves to 15s: social activities work best; aim for three 20-minute sessions of vigorous physical activity each week: walking; dancing; ball games (to foster team spirit). Choose forms of working out which help improve stamina and posture.

Getting physical

This is bound to have an effect on your energy levels, although it also includes manual labour. Exultation makes you glow with satisfaction, from banging home the perfect goal to beating your personal best. The same thing happens when you shut your cupboard door properly after a huge clear-out, packing off all that unwanted stuff to the school jumble sale. The more you engage in some form of activity on a regular basis, daily or even weekly, the more your stamina increases. OK, it's horrible doing something you hate, and many people reckon they loathe exercise, but at the very least, it is good discipline and you can always look forward to the blissful feeling of sheer relief when it's over. There's such a wide choice nowadays, something should suit you, and it doesn't have to take up hours. Yoga, meditation, etc. come under this category; they might not strike you as physically demanding, but it takes hard work to master them.

All in the mind

Energy levels can also be boosted through mental stimulation, that wonderful sensation when you're so wrapped up in something, the outside world, and all its problems, float away. And so many different pursuits, for so many different tastes: chess, crosswords, puzzles, jigsaws, studying. Even thinking, though it's the root of all evil when it comes to low self-esteem, bogging you down when you're sad or angry. Yet when all is well with the world, you're somehow not even conscious of any thoughts going through your mind. When it's questioning, that also does us good, even if it involves taking a deep breath and plunging in, risking admitting to ignorance. Many elderly people claim their liveliness is due to curiosity. But those of us too busy controlling our feelings won't allow ourselves to demonstrate them, even laugh a little or make friends.

The spiritual, too, the by-word and buzz word of today is important for energy. People can be transformed by the effect the arts have on them, making the most of their senses to appreciate everything around them, the wonders of the world. They seek to connect more with other people, and on a deeper level, to enrich their lives. Worth exploring, even for the sceptical, to discover what touches you, or just what you feel most comfortable with.

Body and soul

Like a car needs fuel to run and maintenance to run smoothly, so the body depends on food and fitness. Whatever sport you take up, there are many payoffs: exercise; fun and friendship; a channel for aggression; a means of challenge.

Since participation requires total involvement, it's on a par with meditation; the more you're relaxed, the easier it is to put things into perspective. It's important to be able to loosen up because worry leads to muscle tension. When you express yourself, speaking out brings relief, and consequently relaxes you. Suppressing your feelings makes it difficult to say anything, because it's emotions which result in messages from brain to body, altering breathing and tightening the jaw. However, as long as you're relaxed and flexible, feelings can flow. Practise recognizing tension: lie down, tensing then relaxing each part of your body, working upwards.

Heat is useful, particularly relaxing baths, adding the appropriate aromatherapy oils. Yoga and stretching are both known to be beneficial; done on a regular basis, these improve posture, which makes you appear more confident. Massage is another popular form of relaxation (if a tricky one at first for the truly uptight), one which is as blessed to give as to receive. Massaging somebody aids communication; you're aware of their tension, and whether the massage is having the desired effect or is painful in certain areas. In some cultures, babies are commonly given massage, and even young children can learn the basics. It's also possible to give yourself a massage, more or less.

Alpha to omega?

Meditation is an example of practice making things perfect. Learn how to sink down to alpha level, the deep relaxed state where you're receptive to suggestions and affirmations: take 20 minutes to sit or lie down in a quiet, warm, comfortable room. Don't worry about getting it right, or rush things. Making sure your head and neck are supported, concentrate on breathing though your nose. Breathe out, focusing on words like 'calm' or 'peace', letting your muscles and limbs grow heavy. Let it all go. The sensation of drifting deepens if you slowly count down. Concentrate on a single, simple image or sound, or picture yourself relaxing in your favourite place.

If trying this out in bed, you'll eventually fall asleep. During the daytime, at the end of the session, sit quietly for a moment or so before rejoining the rat race. Learning to accept or adapt whatever happens to you means gaining more satisfaction and becoming more confident. Looking after yourself, you look better and feel better.

Of course, it's much easier to daydream, though that's not helpful if it's what's we opt for rather than trying to bring something about. But safer, after all, because we remain in control; life tends to muck things up. But like physical activity, anything which engages the brain and keeps you fully involved is doing you, and your self-esteem, a power of good.

The art of communication

Learning to communicate properly is excellent for encouraging confidence, though not every family possesses these skills, and there are more problems due to gender and the generation gap. Since about three-quarters of communication is non-verbal, take into account body language and behaviour (actions). Families use cues, codes and short cuts; parents can often tell more from their children's actions, behaviour (particularly when playing) or facial expression, than what they say (see pp. 101–4). One of the main purposes of communication is providing information; a diary or calendar keeps everybody in the know. Allow enough time and arrange regular meetings, whether quick chats or discussions, to give everybody a chance to raise important matters. If a forum seems formal, rather than gathering the family round the dinner table, at least pick a place and time which suits everyone.

Mind reading

Since youngsters aren't as articulate as adults, parents need to check that they really do understand, provide feedback (as positively as possible) and encourage mutual respect. We take it for granted they know what's required of them ('You must have known I was going out'), which undermines their confidence, making them feel they've let us down. It helps to use our superior knowledge, experience and expertise to try to imagine how it is for them; like us they have needs, and feel equally strongly about them. Avoid patronizing them; they're children, neither inferiors nor idiots. No, of course, that's not what you meant, so make it clear. Empathy is one thing, telepathy quite another, and the two of you are not in some supernatural TV series.

Causes of conflict

Efforts to communicate are frequently doomed to failure because nobody likes any form of confrontation. It could involve change, and change is scary, implying always some form of loss. Anticipating an unhappy outcome usually brings this about; believing that the other person is sure to be angry or critical or tearful makes us defensive, and affects them accordingly. Sensitive people should communicate more effectively through their ability to pick up on nuances, but this is wiped out through a tendency to over-react. The confident may be impatient and unsympathetic, whilst the insecure take things personally. But if you deny your feelings, how can you sympathize with others? If you have no self-respect, you won't respect them, and when critical of yourself, you criticize everybody else.

Preparing for the worst

People with poor self-esteem avoid communication: no time; don't feel up to it; can't be bothered; what's the point? But we know that leaving things to drag on makes matters far worse in the long run. Still we put off the evil day, trusting to Fate to rescue us and save us the bother of tackling problems. In fact, having concluded something must be done, coming to a decision makes you feel good, even when forced upon you. Weigh it up: if something really, really gets to you, do you want to have to live with it day in and day out, brood over it, night after sleepless night? Compared with getting through a few admittedly horrendous moments, to make the effort to face some-body? We always grumble: 'I can't stand it a moment longer!', rather than doing anything about it.

Some bad habits aren't easy to dispense with: what sounds OK to you may upset others. That may be their problem, but you could try expressing yourself differently. If it is your problem, it's hard to accept that's how we appear, even unintentionally. But when you accept that something must be done, tempting though it is to get it over with, don't take the other person by surprise, blurt it all out, then disappear before they react. An ambush won't solve anything. Would it work on you? Give some advance warning, without making them (or yourself) apprehensive, then you can both be more open. The other person may have something they'd like to talk to you about, and be grateful you've opened up the channels of communication. Or not. How often do we go on doing things, oblivious to how this is perceived by others? And they're often things for which people have misinterpreted our real reasons.

Communication rules, OK?

Preparation should include a few ground rules. Avoid blame by concentrating on solutions. Stick to the point, and one thing at a time; it's easy to get side-tracked when you haven't had much practice, so agree beforehand to a signal for time out: anything from a five-minute break to having to sleep on it. Let it lie (not fester), so you can gain perspective, absorbing what's been said and reflecting on it, then resume when you're both calmer. Otherwise, you get stuck, saying the same old things and getting nowhere. Communication being a sign of maturity, you wouldn't dream of resorting to name-calling, but don't keep bringing up the past; what's gone is gone. Avoid generalizations: 'You always . . .'; 'I never . . .'. You do – and so do they. Don't worry about memorizing guidelines; you may never need to. It could all go swimmingly, everything resolved, just like that. Or it may end up worse than your worst nightmare. That's unlikely, provided you take precautions for damage limitation; be positive, open and warm. Make it clear you care about them – not because it's 'for their own good'. Aim to end on a positive note, easier to start again, if need be.

Man to man, woman to woman, man to woman . . .

On a one-to-one basis, all our senses are aware, in order to process information. Communication should all be black and white, but it's coloured by the assumptions we make about each other. We should understand that alongside what is real, we are filling in the gaps by guessing. Our view of what is reality may diverge considerably from what you could call the actual reality, and so can the other person's. Matters are improved by offering emotional support: listen and check everything is understood; be patient; don't over-react. It's important to listen closely and ask questions in order to understand better, and to avoid jumping to conclusions. When you're waiting for a phone call which is delayed or never happens, isn't the immediate assumption: they promised to ring, they haven't bothered: proof they don't like me? Even when there's a genuine reason, we continue to apply the same old criteria in this kind of situation, rather than the perfectly logical conclusion.

By taking things personally, we shut down lines of communication. The more this happens, the greater our emotional disability: inability to understand or communicate. Being emotionally unavailable is a means of protection but sends out mixed messages; contradictory meaning and speech. Or we're shut off from the outside world. There's often such discrepancy between what is thought, what is said and what is fact; by hiding our feelings, we keep up appearances, but emotional lies do us no good. If we lose touch with our emotions, we don't know what we are feeling, which affects our self-esteem. Inability to communicate looks as if we have no respect for the other person, and when critical or fearful, you project your feelings onto others, who then reflect them back. Inevitably, it leads to hostility and affects confidence.

The art of reasoning and listening

Two simple solutions to change conflict into communication, but it takes practice for them to be effective.

Sweet reason

Being reasonable is part of being confident; the more you display it, the more your children will be reasonable. Reasoning entails:

- Specific instructions: 'Can you put your book away now, so we can go out?', NOT 'Why do you always let your bookcase get in such a mess? Now I'm going to have start sorting it out so we'll be late and it's all YOUR fault!'
- Explanations: 'Where's your bedtime storybook got to? Why not make some space on the middle shelf here, then you can reach it when you want to look at it yourself?' And point out possible consequences: 'Pity if your book goes missing, we'll never find out what happens to the lonely gnu.'

Reasoning prepares you, working out what's necessary in certain situations. You can allow for a child to be fiercely independent one minute and properly soppy the next.

Listen up

When beset by troubles, we usually turn to the same person. Why? Because they're a good listener; even when they don't happen to agree with you, they're still supportive. Being a good listener is not just hearing what's said, but paying attention so we understand fully, involving eyes, heart and mind, the kind of total absorption you see in babies and young children. That way, we are showing respect, and we're validating them, which is good for self-esteem. Mostly, though, when we're quiet during a conversation, it's not because we're listening, we're too busy formulating our reply.

When asked questions, we ramble on rather than admit we don't know, or assume that the other person will know that we're leading up to it, rather than immediately providing the answer. Poor conversationalists also speak quickly and repeat themselves, often putting on a show to make a good impression rather than sharing the conversation. But once you realize that it takes skill to listen, improvement is immediate, since you can hardly avoid being aware of it during the next conversation. Watch out for:

- Failing to make eye contact; being inattentive; fidgeting (sneaking looks at your watch);
- Poor memory and concentration;
- Interrupting or finishing off sentences;
- Interrogating or interviewing rather than asking questions;
- Disagreeing; making judgements; contradicting;
- Offering: opinion; advice, analysis or interpretation. Or your own experiences.

Reflective listening

The purpose is to unearth the other person's true feelings rather than discuss facts, or how you feel. We all have a dark side, traits we attempt to deny, fearing rejection or disgust, but they may emerge in close relationships, even when both of you are reluctant to discuss it. Sometimes, these revelations are on a need-to-know basis, a question of living with it or changing things. The more sensitive we are, the more we reject the bad bits. It's very painful hearing unpleasant things about ourselves: bad habits; behaviour which is unfair or offputting to others; need to change/mature.

It's easier to acknowledge, once we accept the aim is not to reveal our nasty side, but to improve matters. Keep listening, and let the other person have their say. Don't get upset, springing to your own defence, fighting back or breaking down (a common mechanism; even when furious, the other person will usually have to calm down and take care of you). Reflective listening takes practice; it'll seem odd to you at first, but since the person doing the talking appreciates your undivided attention, it doesn't strike them as unnatural. Set aside about half an hour to allow each of you to have a go, with a few minutes break; maybe 24 hours, if there's conflict or anger.

- Look attentive: the appropriate body language makes people more receptive: open posture; leaning forward; touch; nod; smile; eye contact.
- Repeat what's said paraphrasing not parroting (which can sound like mockery; watch your tone of voice); note verbs used, indicating feelings; concentrate on this, not just their words. As the facts are discussed, explanations emerge and so do underlying feelings.
- Acknowledge what's said by nodding; try not to talk other than murmurs of agreement or consolation. Although silence is important for reflection, let it go on too long and it creates an uncomfortable atmosphere.

You and me

These two schools of thought have an equal number of members; it's often best to stick to 'I' when disclosing your feelings, but opt for that or 'you' depending on the circumstances: 'You must have been upset.' And don't forget, 'I am upset' rather than 'You make me upset.' The intention, however, is the same, to show empathy: 'Oh, I know *just* how you feel!' Trouble is, you don't, or rather, you can't; in a way, it's robbing them of the sympathy they feel they deserve. Everyone hates that response, or assumption, because the focus switches to the other person. Likewise, don't transfer annoyance with somebody onto a third person; that's the effect, even when you think you're calmly explaining about the situation. We're all tempted to anticipate what other people are going to say; when wrong, we end up talking at cross-purposes, although anticipation can show we're on the same wavelength.

Coming to a conclusion: happy endings . . .

A ready reference section for parents to pass on to their children.

Self-confidence? Elementary

Good self-esteem encompasses:

1 Core values: knowing right from wrong; treating others well; coping with pain and difficulties. Healthy attitude: towards power and possessions; health; sexuality; authority; emotions.
2 Sense of responsibility: handling money; decisions; emotions. People with low self-esteem feel safer because they aren't accountable, blaming others, people and circumstances.
3 Ability to solve problems: to think it through, to learn from mistakes, and to forgive yourself.

Other factors

Don't automatically follow the crowd or be dependent on others' views. Fulfilling other people's expectations rather than your own means acting a role: 'I am what I do.' You may appear confident, but you'll never be satisfied. Be honest and truthful; speak out without hurting others, or being hurt by rejection. Aggressive attitudes cut off communication and co-operation. Creating victims of others makes you a victim, swinging round to submission; violent people beg hardest for forgiveness. Work at good relationships, avoiding people with a negative outlook but accept constructive criticism, setting an example. Children model their relationships on yours, so don't be constantly talking about others behind their back. Keep an open house; keep up good communication and offer them unconditional love. Praise them – a compliment a day keeps the doctor at bay.

Maintaining good self-esteem

1 Check your emotions whenever possible: what are you feeling and why do you feel like that? If you say you deserve time to yourself, do you feel guilty? When you're down, nothing helps at first, but you know now how to work at making yourself feel better. Express yourself: say why you feel pleased or annoyed. Say no and stick to it, although that's as hard as hearing it, because of the implications: selfish; mean; unfeeling.
2 List your strengths (even little things) each day: then weaknesses. Are you still trying to live up to your parents' words of wisdom, daily sayings like 'Act your age', passing them on, unquestioning,

to your children? Replace learned responses ('Maybe I'm not always useless') with something positive ('Maybe I am useful').

3 Be more positive: steer clear of negative thoughts, or apply logic: what's the worst that can happen? Is it that bad? Is it that likely? Set yourself attainable goals, affirming your abilities.

4 Begin your day well: use your imagination to plan the next 24 hours, seeing everything going right for you.

5 End the day well: review events and how they could be improved.

6 Help others: from making them feel better with a compliment, to inspiring them.

7 Help yourself: set challenges; learn to persevere; satisfaction is all the greater when you polish off some awful task.

8 Give yourself time to relax: when you're in alpha state and your mind is calmed, think about past problems to try and sort them out. Reframe; looking at anything from different perspectives means you can consider the various motives. Be at peace with yourself, savouring the bliss of a sense of oneness. Contentment is more attainable than happiness, and comes from the inner you; it's not dependent on material things or other people.

9 Reduce apprehension: when facing a hideous ordeal, relive a past success as fully as possible until you experience those same emotions i.e. the buzz. Now choose a code-word ('Steady'; 'Now!') and a significant gesture (crossing your fingers comes to mind) which you then use to generate that particular mind-set. If you loathe 'stage fright', it is possible to eliminate such feelings once you're determined to do so.

Alison loathes giving speeches on behalf of the company, but it's part of her job. She concentrates on recognizing the initial signs of tension, and keeps it in place by relaxing and positive thinking. At a Beatles convention, she's going on stage to address the biggest crowd ever, but whenever the thought crosses her mind, it registers next to nothing on the scale of reaction. She feels even better, because her response is no longer panic.

10 Believe that all will be well, that you can be what you want to be: by picturing good times and bad times, the latter motivates you to avoid pain by concentrating on pleasure.

Those who are more spiritual may prefer the idea of a guardian angel, to guide them and look after them, having only their best interests at heart. When you believe in an afterlife, doesn't it seem likely that those you loved would continue to watch over you? Besides, who gets the blame every time things go wrong? Yet how often do we say 'Thank God!' without meaning it literally?

Now, relax

With some help from the following; alternative remedies help harmonize mind and body: aromatherapy; oils; massage; reflexology; yoga (learning to breathe properly). Aim for a balance between your inner and outer worlds; people with low self-esteem feel trapped inside their head by negative ideas; confident people welcome time spent dwelling within.

Mental aids range from time management to visualization, whilst the emotional include painting, writing or counselling (or talking to friends), releasing frustration or anger: pour out troubles to your favourite teddy bear – even shout at him. For the spiritual, there's meditation, e.g., chanting; prayer; focusing on candles (and you thought lava lamps were neither use nor ornament); reading, looking or listening to something inspirational. Or get physical, improving posture; stretching; exercise; sport. A good way to start is the nutritional: balanced diet; reading up on vitamins and minerals; food, allergies, etc., and the basics are covered by the environmental comfortable furniture: bed, pillows, chairs; use of colour; feng shui.

And finally

It's said that about one-fifth of success is down to brain power and abilities, the rest comes from creativity and perseverance. When you believe in yourself and others believe in you, your confidence blossoms, and so will your children. You can do it.

Useful addresses

Alcohol

Alcoholics Anonymous
PO Box 1
Stonebow House
Stonebow
York YO1 7NJ
Tel. (24 hr): 0845 769 7555

Bullying

Anti-Bullying Campaign
185 Tower Bridge Road
London SE1 2UF
Tel.: 020 7378 1446

Fact sheet available. SAE please.

Kidscape
2 Grosvenor Gardens
London SW1V 0DH
Tel.: 020 7730 3300

Booklets and literature available. Preventing child abuse and bullying.

Childcare

Daycare Trust
Shoreditch Town Hall Annexe
380 Old Street
London EC1V 9LT
Tel.: 020 7739 2866
Fax: 020 7739 5579

Advice on quality childcare.

Kids' Clubs Network
Bellerive House
3 Muirfield Crescent
London E14 9SZ
Tel.: 020 7512 2100

National body for out-of-school childcare for children 5 – 12.

The National Early Years Network
77 Holloway Road
London N7 8JZ
Tel.: 020 7607 9573

For details of local services for under-eights.

Pre-School Learning Alliance
69 Kings Cross Road
London WC1X 9LL
Tel.: 020 7833 0991
Fax: 020 7837 4942

Email: pla@pre-school.org.uk
www.pre-school.org.uk

Information about voluntarily run UK playgroups.

Children

Childline
Freepost 1111
London N1 0BR
Helpline (24 hr): 0800 1111

For children and young people only.

Cry-sis
BM Cry-sis
London WC1N 3XX
Tel.: 020 7404 5011

Support for parents whose children cry excessively.

National Children's Bureau
8 Wakley Street
London EC1V 7QE
Tel.: 020 7843 6000

www.ncb.org.uk

Leaflets and books.

The Children's Society
Edward Rudolf House
Margery Street
London WC1X 0JL
Tel.: 020 7837 4299

www.the-children's-society.org.uk

Counselling

British Association for Counselling
1 Regent Place
Rugby CV21 2PJ
Information line: 01788 57 8328

www.counselling.co.uk

Institute of Family Therapy
24 – 32 Stephenson Way
London NW1 2HX
Tel.: 020 7391 9150

National Association for Mental Health (MIND)
Granta House
15 – 19 Broadway
Stratford
London E15 4B2
Tel.: 020 8519 2122
Information line: 020 8522 1728

Information and services, including leaflets, about a range of mental
health problems.

Saneline
1st Floor, Cityside House
40 Adler Street
London E1
Tel. (12pm to 2am, all year): 0845 767 8000

Youth Crime Section
National Association for the Care and Resettlement of Offenders
(NACRO)
159 Clapham Road
London SW9 0PU
Tel.: 020 7582 6500

Disability

Contact-a-Family
170 Tottenham Court Road
London W1P 0HA
Helpline: 020 7383 3555

Information and support for families with children who have special
needs.

Disability Alliance
Universal House
88 – 94 Wentworth Street
London E1 7SA
Tel.: 020 7247 8776

Helpline for benefits advice (Mon & Wed, 2 – 4pm): 020 7247 8763

www.disabilityalliance.org.uk

Domestic Violence

Women's Aid Federation
National Helpline (24 hr): 08457 02 3468

Drugs

ADFAM National
Tel. (Mon. 10am – 5pm; Tues. 10am – 7pm; Wed. – Fri. 10am – 5pm):
Helpline 020 7928 8900.
Admin. 020 7928 8898

Confidential support and information for families and friends of drug
users.

Drugscope
Waterbridge House
32–36 Loman Street
London SE1 0EE
Tel.: 020 7928 1211

Provides information. Send large SAE for publications list.

Drugs in Schools Adviser
Tel.: 0808 800 0800

Families Anonymous
The Doddington and Rollo Community Association
Charlotte Despard Avenue
Battersea
London SW11 5JE
Tel. (Mon. to Fri. 1pm – 4pm; evenings & weekends): 020 7498 4680

Free and confidential advice at any time. Advises on local support for families.

Release
388 Old Street
London EC1V 9LT
Tel.: 020 7729 9904
Emergency number (outside normal working hours): 020 7603 6854

A range of services, including legal advice for drug users, their families and friends.

The National Drugs Helpline
Tel.: 0800 77 6600

Eating Disorders

National Centre for Eating Disorders
54 New Road
Esher
Surrey KT10 9NU
Tel.: 01372 46 9493
Fax: 01372 46 9550

Education

Education Otherwise
PO Box 7420
London N9 9SG
Tel.: 0870 730 0074

National Association for Gifted Children (NAGC)
540 Elder Gate
Milton Keynes MK9 1LR
Tel.: 01908 67 3677

Families and Stepfamilies

Parentline Plus
520 Highgate Studios
53 – 79 Highgate Road
London NW5 1TL

Tel.: 020 7284 5500
Helpline: 0808 800 2222
Text phone: 0800 783 6783

Email: centraloffice@parentlineplus.org.uk
www.parentlineplus.org.uk

Advice and information for all people in a parenting role.

Gambling

Gam-Anon
PO Box 88
London SW10 0EU
Tel.: 020 7384 3040

For partners and families of compulsive gamblers.

GamCare
Suite 1, Catherine House
25–27 Catherine Place
Westminster
London SW1E 6DU
Helpline (10am – 10pm): 0845 600 0133

Smoking

ASH (Action on Smoking and Health)
102 Clifton Street
London EC2A 4HW
Tel.: 020 7739 5902

www.ash.org.uk

National Smoking Helpline: 0800 169 0169

Quit
Tel.: 0207 388 5775

Quitline
Tel. (seven days, 12pm – 9pm): 0800 00 2200

Solvents

Re-Solv (The Society for the Prevention of Solvent and Volatile
Substance Abuse)
30A High Street

Stone
Staffordshire ST15 8AW
Tel.: (9am – 5pm, Mon. to Fri.): 0808 800 2345

www.re-solv.org

Publishes leaflets, booklets & videos; puts you in touch with local
agencies.

Teenagers

Brook Advisory Centre
Tottenham Court Road Centre
233 Tottenham Court Road
London W1P 9AE
Tel.: 0800 018 5023

National Youth Agency
Telephone duty desk: 0116 285 3700

www.nya.org,uk

Information database for young people.

The Trust for the Study of Adolescence (TSA)
23 New Road
Brighton
East Sussex BN1 1WZ
Tel.: 01273 69 3311
Fax: 01273 67 9907

Catalogues, books, videos, conferences.

Work

Parents at Work
45 Beech Street
Barbican
London EC2Y 8AD
Tel.: 020 7628 3578
Helpline for low income families
(Wed & Fri, 11am – 2pm; Thurs 6am – 9pm): 020 7628 2128
Helpline for parents of disabled children
(Wed – Fri 9.30am – 1pm; and 2pm – 4.30pm): 020 7588 0802

The voice of working parents – campaigns to improve the quality of life
for working parents and their children, including single parents. Regular
newsletters, various fact sheets and publications, etc.

Further reading

Improving self-esteem

Adult

Elaine N. Aron, *The Highly Sensitive Person*. Thorsons, London, 1999.
Melanie Fennell, *Overcoming Low Self-Esteem: A Self-Help Guide Using Cognitive Behavioural Techniques*, Robinson, London, 1999.
Lynda Field, *Creating Self-Esteem: A Practical Guide to Realizing Your True Worth*, Element, Dorset, 1998.
Dr Paul Hauck, *Hold Your Head Up High*, Sheldon Press, London, 1997.
Dr Paul Hauck, *How to Stand up for Yourself*. Sheldon Press, London, 1990.
Rex Johnson and David Swindley, *Creating Confidence: The Secrets of Self Esteem*, Element, Dorset, 1999.

Children

Sylvia Clare, *Raising the Successful Child: How to Encourage your Child on the Road to Emotional and Learning Competence*, How to Books, Oxford, 1998.
Jennifer Day, *Children Believe Everything You Say: Creating Self-esteem with Children*, Element, Dorset, 1997.
Dr Wayne W. Dyer, *What Do You Really Want For Your Children?*, Arrow, London, 1997.
Anne and Denis Lawrence, *Self-Esteem and your Child: A Guide to Happy Parenting*, Minerva Press, London, 1996.
Gael Lindenfield, *Confident Children: A Parent's Guide to Helping Children Feel Good about Themselves*, Thorsons, London, 1994.
Clare Shaw, *Help Your Child be Confident*, Headway, Hodder & Stoughton, London, 1996.
Barbara Sher, *Self-Esteem Games: 300 Fun Activities that make Children Feel Good about Themselves*, John Wiley & Sons Inc., Chichester, 1998.

Parenting

Steve Biddulph, *Raising Boys*, Thorsons, London, 1998.
Steve Biddulph, *The Secret of Happy Children*, Thorsons, London, 1998.
Brenda Houghton, *The Good Child: How to Instil a Sense of Right and Wrong in your Child*, Headline, London, 1998.
Lucky Duck Publishing, *Even Better Parents*, Bristol, 1997. Training Pack: video, manual, etc.
Clare Shaw, *The 5-Minute Mum: Time Management for Busy Parents*, Hodder & Stoughton Positive Parenting series, London, 1995.
Dr Stanley Turecki with Leslie Tonner, *The Difficult Child: How to Understand and Cope with your Temperamental 2–6 Year Old*, Piatkus, London, 1995.

Education

Ken Adams, *Bring Out the Genius in Your Child*, Ward Lock, London, 1997.

Jennie and Lance Lindon, *Help Your Child Through School*, Hodder & Stoughton, London, 1994.

Work

Sally Garratt, *Manage Your Time*, HarperCollins, London, 1994.

Eileen Gillibrand and Jenny Mosley, *When I Go to Work, I Feel Guilty*, Thorsons, London, 1997.

Elizabeth Perle McKenna, *When Work Doesn't Work Anymore*, Simon & Schuster, London, 1997.

General

Bereavement

Sylvia Murphy, *Dealing with a Death in the Family*, How to Books, Oxford, 1996.

Law

Aviva Golden, *The Daily Telegraph Guide to Parenting and The Law*, Harper-Collins, London, 1998.

Health

Adults

Denise Brown, *Massage*, Hodder & Stoughton Teach Yourself series, London, 1997.

Dr Richard Gillett, *Overcoming Depression*, Dorling Kindersley, London, 1992.

Cathy Hopkins, *101 Short Cuts to Relaxation*, Bloomsbury, London, 1997.

Judith Jackson, *The Magic of Well-Being: A Sensory Self-Discovery Programme for a Fulfilling Life*, Dorling Kindersley, London, 1997.

Joan Radford, *The Complete Book of Family Aromatherapy*, Foulsham, Berkshire, 1993.

Maxine Tobias and John Patrick Sullivan, *The Complete Stretching Book*, Dorling Kindersley, London, 1997.

Psychology

James W. Jones, *In the Middle of This Road We Call Our Life*, Thorson, London, 1995.

M. Peck, *The Road Less Travelled*, Arrow, London, 1978.

Young People

Alcohol

R. Armitage, *Let's Discuss Drinking*, Wayland, London, 1987.

John Coleman and Coralie Tiffin, *Teenagers and Alcohol*, TSA Publishing Ltd, Brighton, 1993.

Drugs

Paul Francis, *Help your Kids Stay Drug-Free*, HarperCollins, London, 1999.

Charles Rubin, *Don't Let Your Kids Kill You: A Guide for Parents of Drug and Alcohol Addicted Children*, Element, Dorset, 1997.

Yvette Solomon and John Coleman, *Dealing with Substance Abuse*, Wayland, London, 1995.

Eating Disorders

Claire Beeken with Rosanna Greenstreet, *My Body, My Enemy: My Thirteen Year Battle with Anorexia Nervosa*, Thorsons, London, 1997.

Sandra Susan Friedman, *When Girls feel Fat: Helping Girls through Adolescence*, HarperCollins, London, 1997.

Kate Haycock, *Dealing with Eating Disorders*, Wayland, London, 1994.

Teenage Pregnancy

Pamela De Salvo and Tricia Skuse, *The Really Helpful Directory: Services for Pregnant Teenagers and Young Parents*, TSA Publishing Ltd, Brighton, 1993.

Dr Frances Peck, *Handbook for Young Mothers*, Rainer Foundation, London, 1993. NB. This is available free at some clinics or agencies.

Relationships

Body Language

Allan Pease, *Body Language*, Sheldon Press, London, 1997.

Susan Quilliam, *Child Watching: A Parent's Guide to Children's Body Language*, Ward Lock, London, 1994.

Communication

Dr Windy Dryden and Jack Gordon, *How to Cope with Difficult Parents*, Sheldon Press, London, 1995.

Dr Susan Forward with Donna Frazier, *Emotional Blackmail*, Bantam Press, London, 1997.

Don Gabor, *How to Start a Conversation and Make Friends*, Sheldon Press, London, 1997.

Wendy Grant, *Resolving Conflicts: How to Turn Conflict into Cooperation*, Element, Dorset, 1997.

Thomas A. Harris, MD, *I'm OK – You're OK*, Pan, London, 1973.

Dr Paul Hauck, *How to Cope with People who Drive you Crazy*, Sheldon Press, London, 1998.

Alan Houel with Christian Godefroy, *How to Cope with Difficult People*, Sheldon Press, London 1997.

Elizabeth Mapstone, *War of Words: Women and Men Arguing*, Chatto & Windus, London, 1998.

Douglas Stone, Bruce Patton and Sheila Heen, *Difficult Conversations: How to Discuss what Matters Most*, Michael Joseph, London, 1999.

Children

Bereavement

Rosemary Wells, *Helping Children Cope with Grief*, Sheldon Press, London, 1988.

Bullying

Michele Elliott, *101 Ways to Deal with Bullying*, Hodder & Stoughton, London, 1997.

Sarah Lawson, *Helping Children Cope with Bullying*, Sheldon Press, London, 1995.

Dr John Pearce, *Fighting, Teasing and Bullying*, Thorsons, London, 1989.

George Robinson and Barbara Maines, *Crying for Help*, Lucky Duck Publishing, Bristol, 1997.

Divorce

Anne Charlish, *Caught in the Middle: Helping Children to Cope with Separation and Divorce*, Ward Lock, London, 1997.

Rosemary Wells, *Helping Children Cope with Divorce*, Sheldon Press, London, 1997.

Teenagers

Parents

Helen Braid (ed.), *A Stranger at My Table: Women Write about Mothering Adolescents*, The Women's Press, London, 1997.

Elizabeth Fenwick and Dr Tony Smith, *Adolescence: The Survival Guide for Parents and Teenagers*, Dorling Kindersley, London, 1993.

Debi Roker and John Coleman, *Teenagers in the Family*, Hodder & Stoughton, London, 1995.

Problems

Emma Haughton, *Dealing with Peer Pressure*, Wayland, London, 1995.

Barbara Lloyd and Kevin Lucas *et al.*, *Smoking in Adolescence: Images and Identities*, Routledge, London, 1998.

Martin Plant and Moira Plant, *Risk-Takers: Alcohol, Drugs, Sex and Youth*, Tavistock/Routledge, London, 1992.

School Information Packs, Carole Baldock, Knight & Bishop, Huddersfield, 1996 onwards:

Aiming for 'As'
Bully Off! I: Victims?
Bully Off! II: Villains?
Money Management for Teenagers I: Income
Money Management for Teenagers II: Outgoings

Teenage Pregnancy I: Making the Choices
Teenage Pregnancy II: Keeping the Baby.

Books for young people

Fiction

Susan Albertson, *Between the Lines*, Armada, London. (Theme: friendship)
Judy Blume, *It's Not the End of the World*, Piper. (Theme: divorce)
Steven Levenkron, *The Best Little Girl in the World*, Puffin, London. (Theme: anorexia)
J.D. Salinger, *The Catcher in the Rye*. (Theme: problems of adolescence)

Non-fiction

Karen Bryant-Mole, *Splitting Up* and *Step Families*, Wayland, London, 1994.
Jill Dawson, *How Do I Look?*, Virago, London, 1991.

Index